GoodFood
MAGAZINE

D0247748

101 CHOCOLATE TREATS

5 7 9 10 8 6 4

Published in 2007 by BBC Books,
an imprint of Ebury Publishing
A Random House Group Company

Copyright © Woodlands Books 2007
All photographs © *BBC Good Food Magazine* 2007
All the recipes contained in this book first appeared in
BBC Good Food Magazine.

The Random House Group Limited Reg. No. 954009

Addresses for companies within the Random House Group can be found
at www.randomhouse.co.uk

A CIP catalogue record for this book is available from the British Library

The Random House Group Limited makes every effort to ensure that
the papers used in our books are made from trees that have been legally
sourced from well-managed and credibly certified forests. Our paper
procurement policy can be found on www.randomhouse.co.uk

Set in Bookman Old Style and Helvetica
Printed and bound in Italy by LEGO SpA
Colour origination by Dot Gradations Ltd, UK

Commissioning Editor: Nicky Ross
Project Editor: Helena Caldon
Designer: Kathryn Gammon
Production Controller: Katharine Hockley

ISBN: 9780563539285

101 CHOCOLATE TREATS
TRIED-AND-TESTED RECIPES

Editor
Jeni Wright

Contents

Introduction

Who doesn't love chocolate? No one at *BBC Good Food Magazine* that's for sure… and we bet you're the same. In this lavishly illustrated volume of over one hundred recipes – each with chocolate as its star ingredient – you'll find there's something for everyone. There are recipes for the confirmed chocoholic who'll find any excuse to indulge in their favourite food, or for those who reserve their cravings for the occasional treat.

There are plenty of easy-to-make cakes and cookies to tempt you, and there's a huge choice of dazzling desserts for dinner parties and other special occasions. There's also a section on hot chocolate puddings (the ultimate in comfort food), and when you're in a hurry you can dip into the chapter of quick and easy recipes; none of which takes more than half an hour to prepare. Last, but not least, don't miss the handful of treats at the back of the book – we all need to spoil ourselves once in a while.

All the recipes have been tried and tested in the *Good Food* kitchen, which means you can be sure of successful results every time, and we've given nutritional breakdowns as well, so you can see at a glance what each dish contains. If the calorie count looks high, remember: the occasional indulgence will make you feel good, and if you use top-quality chocolate it can do you good too!

Jeni Wright
BBC Good Food Magazine

Conversion tables

NOTES ON THE RECIPES
• Eggs are medium in the UK and Australia (large in America) unless stated otherwise.
• Wash all fresh produce before preparation.
• Recipes contain nutritional analyses for 'sugar', which means the total sugar content including all natural sugars in the ingredients, or 'added sugar' – which is sugar added to the recipe.

APPROXIMATE WEIGHT CONVERSIONS
• All the recipes in this book list both imperial and metric measurements. Conversions are approximate and have been rounded up or down. Follow one set of measurements only; do not mix the two.
• Cup measurements, which are used by cooks in Australia and America, have not been listed here as they vary from ingredient to ingredient. Please use kitchen scales to measure dry/solid ingredients.

OVEN TEMPERATURES

Gas	°C	Fan °C	°F	Oven temp.
¼	110	90	225	Very cool
½	120	100	250	Very cool
1	140	120	275	Cool or slow
2	150	130	300	Cool or slow
3	160	140	325	Warm
4	180	160	350	Moderate
5	190	170	375	Moderately hot
6	200	180	400	Fairly hot
7	220	200	425	Hot
8	230	210	450	Very hot
9	240	220	475	Very hot

SPOON MEASURES
• Spoon measurements are level unless otherwise specified.
• 1 teaspoon = 5ml
• 1 tablespoon = 15ml
• 1 Australian tablespoon = 20ml (cooks in Australia should measure 3 teaspoons where 1 tablespoon is specified in a recipe)

APPROXIMATE LIQUID CONVERSIONS

metric	imperial	AUS	US
50ml	2fl oz	¼ cup	¼ cup
125ml	4fl oz	½ cup	½ cup
175ml	6fl oz	¾ cup	¾ cup
225ml	8fl oz	1 cup	1 cup
300ml	10fl oz/½ pint	½ pint	1¼ cups
450ml	16fl oz	2 cups	2 cups/1 pint
600ml	20fl oz/1 pint	1 pint	2½ cups
1 litre	35fl oz/1¾ pints	1¾ pints	1 quart

A scrumptious yet sophisticated chocolate and coffee cake
that you'll go nuts about.

Mocha Hazelnut Cake

150g bar dark chocolate, chopped
4 tbsp strong black coffee
175g/6oz butter, softened
175g/6oz caster sugar
5 large eggs, lightly beaten
100g/4oz ground hazelnuts
100g/4oz self-raising flour, sifted
with 1 tsp baking powder

FOR THE FILLING
100g bar dark chocolate, chopped
50g/2oz butter, diced
3 tbsp strong black coffee
4 tbsp double cream
50g/2oz icing sugar, sifted
50g/2oz toasted hazelnuts, roughly
chopped

Takes 1½ hours, plus cooling and
chilling • Cuts into 12 slices

1 Preheat oven to 180°C/Gas 4/fan oven
160°C. Butter and line a 20cm/8in round
cake tin. Melt the chocolate with the coffee.
2 Beat the butter and sugar until fluffy. Slowly
beat in the eggs, then fold in the chocolate,
hazelnuts and flour mix. Pour into the tin and
bake for 45–55 minutes until firm. Cool for
5 minutes, then turn out and cool on a rack.
3 Make the filling. Gently heat the chocolate,
butter, coffee and cream in a pan and stir
until smooth. Remove from the heat and stir in
the icing sugar. Cool, then chill for 1–2 hours
until spreadable. Stir occasionally.
4 Cut the cake in half horizontally. Spread
one half with filling and scatter over half the
hazelnuts. Cover with the other cake half,
spread with the remaining filling, and scatter
the hazelnuts around the edge.

• Per slice 492 kcalories, protein 7g, carbohydrate 40g,
fat 35g, saturated fat 16g, fibre 2g, added sugar 33g,
salt 0.59g

A simple yet stunning cake that could also be served as a delicious dessert.

Chocolate-dipped Cherry Cake

150g/5oz milk chocolate
175g/6oz self-raising flour, sifted
with 1 tsp baking powder
140g/5oz golden caster sugar
140g/5oz very soft, slightly
salted butter
3 large eggs
3 tbsp milk
1 ripe banana, peeled and mashed

TO FINISH
450g/1lb cherries, half of which
pitted and halved
225g/8oz white chocolate, melted
150ml/¼ pint crème fraîche

Takes 1¼ hours, plus cooling • Cuts
into 10 generous slices

1 Preheat oven to 180°C/Gas 4/fan oven 160°C. Butter and base-line two 20cm/8in sandwich tins. Grate two-thirds of the milk chocolate and chop the rest.
2 Beat the flour and sugar with the butter, eggs and milk until light and fluffy. Fold in the chocolate and the banana. Divide between the tins and bake for 25–30 minutes until springy. Cool for 5 minutes then turn out on to a rack. Leave until cold.
3 Dip half the cherries in the melted white chocolate then place on a foil-lined baking sheet. Stir the crème fraîche into the remaining melted chocolate. Cool. Transfer half to a bowl and stir in the halved cherries.
4 Sandwich the cakes with the cherry chocolate cream and top with the chocolate cream. Decorate with the dipped cherries.

• Per slice 501 kcalories, protein 8g, carbohydrate 55g, fat 29g, saturated fat 14g, fibre 1g, added sugar 31g, salt 0.77g

The ultimate cake for chocoholics, indulgently topped
with chocolate curls.

Best-ever Chocolate Cake

225g/8oz dark chocolate (about 60%
cocoa solids), chopped
200g/8oz butter, diced
1 tbsp instant coffee granules
85g/3oz self-raising flour
85g/3oz plain flour
¼ tsp bicarbonate of soda
200g/7oz light muscovado sugar
200g/7oz golden caster sugar
25g/1oz cocoa powder
3 medium eggs, beaten
5 tbsp buttermilk
grated chocolate or curls, to decorate

FOR THE GANACHE
284ml carton double cream
(pouring type)
2 tbsp golden caster sugar
225g/8oz dark chocolate, chopped

Takes 2 hours, plus cooling •
Cuts into 14 slices

1 Preheat oven to 160°C/Gas 3/fan oven
140°C. Butter and line a 20cm/8in round and
7.5cm/3in deep cake tin. Melt the chocolate
with the butter, coffee and 125ml/4fl oz water.
2 Mix together the flours, soda, sugars and
cocoa. Mix the eggs with the buttermilk. Stir
the chocolate and egg mixes into the flour
until smooth and quite runny. Pour into the tin
and bake for 1½ hours, until the top is firm.
Leave to cool in the tin, turn out on to a rack.
When completely cool, cut into three layers.
3 Make the ganache. Scald the cream and
sugar in a pan, pour over the chocolate in
a bowl and stir until melted and smooth.
4 Sandwich the layers with ganache. Pour the
rest over the cake, smooth with a palette knife
and top with chocolate curls.

• Per slice 541 kcalories, protein 6g, carbohydrate 55g,
fat 35g, saturated fat 20g, fibre 2g, added sugar 40g,
salt 0.51g

A delicious and simple teatime treat that children will love
to help you make and eat!

Chocolate-fudge Easter Cakes

FOR THE CAKES
140g/5oz butter, softened
140g/5oz golden caster sugar
3 medium eggs
100g/4oz self-raising flour
25g/1oz cocoa powder, sifted

TO FINISH
85g/3oz milk chocolate, chopped
85g/3oz butter, softened
140g/5oz icing sugar, sifted
2 × 35g packets white
chocolate Maltesers
mini foil-wrapped chocolate eggs

Takes 30 minutes, plus cooling •
Makes 16

1 Preheat oven to 190°C/Gas 5/fan oven
170°C. Put 16 gold cases into a bun tin.
2 Tip all the ingredients for the cakes into a
bowl and beat for 2 minutes with an electric
mixer until smooth. Divide among the cases
so they are two-thirds full, then bake for
12–15 minutes until risen. Cool on a rack.
3 Melt the milk chocolate in a bowl over
a pan of hot water (or microwave on High
for 1 minute). Cream the butter and icing
sugar together, then beat in the melted
chocolate to make a smooth frosting. Spread
on the cakes, then decorate with Maltesers
and chocolate eggs.

• Per cake 274 kcalories, protein 3g, carbohydrate
31g, fat 16g, saturated fat 9g, fibre 1g, sugar 25g,
salt 0.43g

A chocolate delight that is not for the faint-hearted.
A truly decadent dinner-party dessert.

Decadent Truffle Torte

250g/9oz dark chocolate, chopped
2 tbsp golden syrup
568ml carton double cream
4 tsp instant coffee granules,
dissolved in boiling water, cooled
1 tsp ground cinnamon
cocoa powder, for dusting

Takes 50–60 minutes, plus chilling •
Cuts into 12 small slices

1 Line an 18cm/7in springform cake tin with cling film, smoothing out as many wrinkles as possible. Melt the chocolate with the syrup and a quarter of the cream. Leave to cool.
2 In a large bowl, whip the remaining cream with the coffee and cinnamon until it holds its shape. Fold in the cooled chocolate mix evenly with a large metal spoon, then pour into the tin and level the surface. Chill for at least an hour until firm, or leave overnight.
3 Unclip and remove the side of the tin, then peel the cling film away from the side of the cake. Invert a serving plate over the cake and turn the cake upside down on to it. Remove the tin base and cling film. Dust all over with cocoa powder and serve in thin slices.

• Per slice 331 kcalories, protein 2g, carbohydrate 17g, fat 29g, saturated fat 18g, fibre 1g, added sugar 15g, salt 0.09g

Oranges and dark chocolate make a wonderful combination, and here an orange adds a zesty twist to a chocolate cake.

Dark Chocolate and Orange Cake

1 Seville orange
3 large eggs
280g/10oz caster sugar
240ml/8½fl oz sunflower oil
100g/4oz dark chocolate, melted
and cooled
250g/9oz plain flour
25g/1oz cocoa powder
1½ tsp baking powder
candied orange zest, to decorate

FOR THE GANACHE
225ml/8fl oz double cream
225g/8oz dark chocolate, chopped

Takes 2 hours, plus cooling •
Cuts into 10 slices

1 Pierce a skewer through the orange. Cook in boiling water for 30 minutes until soft, drain and whiz in a food processor until smooth.
2 Preheat oven to 180°C/Gas 4/fan oven 160°C. Grease and line a 23cm/9in round tin.
3 Lightly beat the eggs, sugar and oil. Slowly beat in the puréed orange, discarding any pips, then stir in the chocolate. Sift in the flour, cocoa and baking powders. Mix and pour into the tin. Bake for 55–60 minutes or until springy to the touch. Cool for 10 minutes, then turn out on to a rack to cool completely.
4 Bring the cream to the boil and pour it over the chocolate in a bowl. Leave for 2 minutes. Stir until smooth then leave until firm (up to 1½ hours). Swirl the ganache over the cake and decorate with orange zest.

• Per slice 703 kcalories, protein 7g, carbohydrate 73g, fat 45g, saturated fat 16g, fibre 2g, added sugar 51g, salt 0.42g

Make children's Hallowe'en parties a real hoot with these fun
and tasty little cakes.

Hooting Hallowe'en Owls

FOR THE CAKES
280g/10oz butter, softened
280g/10oz golden caster sugar
200g/7oz self-raising flour, minus
1 rounded tbsp
1 rounded tbsp cocoa powder
6 medium eggs

TO FINISH
200g/7oz butter, softened
280g/10oz icing sugar, sifted
1 tube orange ready-to-use icing
1 small packet Maltesers
1 tube chocolate M&Ms minis (just
the brown sweets) or mini
chocolate buttons
1 tub jelly diamonds (just the
orange ones)

Takes 45 minutes, plus cooling •
Makes 12

1 Preheat oven to 190°C/Gas 5/fan oven 170°C. Line a 12-cup muffin tin with brown muffin cases. Beat the cake ingredients to a smooth batter and spoon into the cases, almost filling them to the top. You may have a little left over. Bake for 20–25 minutes until risen and spongy. Cool on a rack.
2 Beat the butter and icing sugar until smooth. Slice off the very tops of the cakes and cut each piece in half. Spread a generous layer of icing over each cake.
3 Working on one cake at a time, squirt a pea-sized blob of orange icing on to two Maltesers and use to fix a brown M&M on each. Sit the eyes, two pieces of cake top (curved edge up) and a jelly diamond on the icing to make an owl.

• Per cake 615 kcalories, protein 6g, carbohydrate 68g, fat 38g, saturated fat 23g, fibre 1g, added sugar 54g, salt 1.06g

Drizzling a criss-cross pattern with white and milk chocolate gives this simple cake a sophisticated look.

Chocolate Drizzle Torte

140g/5oz dark chocolate (preferably 70% cocoa solids), chopped
100g/4oz butter, diced
6 large eggs, separated
140g/5oz ground almonds
85g/3oz golden caster sugar

FOR THE GANACHE
225g/8oz dark chocolate (preferably 70% cocoa solids), chopped
200ml/7fl oz double cream
25g/1oz butter, softened

TO DECORATE
50g/2oz milk chocolate, melted
50g/2oz white chocolate, melted

Takes 1 hour 20 minutes, plus cooling
• Cuts into 12 slices

1 Preheat oven to 170°C/Gas 3/fan oven 150°C. Butter and line a 20cm/8in cake tin. Melt the chocolate and butter together, stirring until smooth. Cool for 5 minutes, then stir in the egg yolks and almonds.
2 Whisk the egg whites to soft peaks, then gradually whisk in the sugar until stiff peaks form. Stir a spoonful of egg whites into the chocolate mix, fold in the rest, then spoon into the tin. Bake for 30–35 minutes until risen and just firm. Cool in the tin, turn out.
3 Put the chocolate for the ganache in a bowl. Scald the cream, pour on to the chocolate and stir until melted, then add the butter and stir until smooth. Cool slightly.
4 Cut the cake horizontally in half, sandwich with a third of the ganache and cover with the rest. Drizzle with the melted chocolate.

• Per slice 491 kcalories, protein 9g, carbohydrate 31g, fat 38g, saturated fat 4g, fibre 2g, added sugar 29g, salt 0.3g

Once the Christmas tree is decorated, let the children loose on this cake with chocolate drizzle and sparkling silver and gold balls.

Festive Chocolate Cake

225g/8oz butter, softened
300g/10oz caster sugar
4 medium eggs, beaten
finely grated zest of 1 large orange
450g/1lb self-raising flour, sifted
5 tbsp milk

TO DECORATE
2 × 100g bars milk chocolate, chopped
100g bar dark chocolate, chopped
100g bar white chocolate, chopped
edible silver or gold balls

Takes 1 hour, plus cooling •
Cuts into 12 slices

1 Preheat oven to 180°C/Gas 4/fan oven 160°C. Butter and base-line two round cake tins, 24cm/9½in and 18cm/7in.
2 Beat the butter and sugar until light and creamy, then gradually beat in the eggs and zest. Add some flour to prevent separating. Fold in the remaining flour and the milk, then divide between the tins and smooth the tops.
3 Bake the small cake for 30–35 minutes and the large cake for 40–45 minutes, until golden and springy. Cool in the tins, then turn out on to racks and peel off the paper.
4 Melt the milk and dark chocolate together, and the white chocolate separately. Dab some chocolate in the middle of the large cake and set the small cake on top. Decorate and leave to set.

• Per slice 569 kcalories, protein 8g, carbohydrate 76g, fat 28g, saturated fat 16g, fibre 2g, added sugar 45g, salt 0.8g

Save yourself time and prepare the meringues and cake ahead so you can simply fill them and dust with icing sugar on the day.

Chocolate Crunch Gâteau

50g/2oz cocoa powder
225ml/8fl oz hot water
100g/4oz butter, softened
280g/10oz caster sugar
2 large eggs, beaten
175g/6oz self-raising flour
½ tsp bicarbonate of soda

FOR THE MERINGUE
2 large egg whites
100g/4oz caster sugar

TO FINISH
284ml carton double cream, softly whipped
57g tube Rolos, roughly chopped (optional)
icing sugar, for dusting

Takes 1 hour, plus cooling •
Cuts into 12 slices

1 Preheat oven to 160°C/Gas 3/fan oven 140°C. Butter and line two 20cm/8in round tins. Mix the cocoa and water until smooth. Cream the butter and sugar, then whisk in the eggs. Pour the cocoa mix over, sift the flour and soda on top, and fold to make a smooth batter. Divide between the tins.
2 Make the meringue. Whisk the egg whites to stiff peaks. Whisk in half the sugar until glossy, then fold in the rest. Spoon the meringue over the cakes, leaving a 2cm/¾in border. Bake for 40 minutes until the meringue is crisp and the cakes cooked. Leave in the tins for 5 minutes, then cool on a rack with the meringue uppermost.
3 With the meringue on top, sandwich the cakes with the cream and Rolo mix (if using).

• Per slice 406 kcalories, protein 5g, carbohydrate 48g, fat 23g, saturated fat 14g, fibre 1g, sugar 36g, salt 0.6g

Blow your guests away with this chocolate explosion, and give it
a fiery twist with glowing-orange candied fruits.

Rippled Chocolate Bombe

150g bar dark chocolate (at least
70% cocoa solids), chopped
250g/9oz butter, softened
225g/8oz golden caster sugar
4 large eggs
225g/8oz plain flour
2 tsp baking powder
100g/4oz ground almonds
3 tbsp cocoa powder
1 tbsp milk
2 tsp vanilla extract

TO FINISH
150g bar dark chocolate (at least
70% cocoa solids), chopped
142ml carton double cream
sliced candied fruits

Takes 2 hours, plus cooling and
chilling • Cuts into 12 slices

1 Preheat oven to 160°C/Gas 3/fan oven
140°C. Grease a 1.7 litre/3 pint mixing bowl
and line the bottom with greaseproof paper.
2 Melt the chocolate with 25g/1oz butter.
Beat the rest of the butter with the sugar,
eggs, flour, baking powder and 85g/3oz
almonds. Put 350g/12oz of this into a bowl,
stir in the cocoa and milk. Stir the vanilla and
remaining almonds into the plain mix.
3 Spread a little vanilla mix in the bottom of
the prepared bowl. Top with some cocoa mix,
then a little melted chocolate in the centre.
Repeat layers, then swirl with a skewer.
Bake for 1½ hours or until cake is cooked.
Cool, then invert on to a plate.
4 Melt the other chocolate bar with the
cream. Chill for 30 minutes, stirring until it
holds its shape. Swirl over the cake.

• Per slice 584 kcalories, protein 9g, carbohydrate
55g, fat 38g, saturated fat 20g, fibre 2g, added sugar
37g, salt 0.46g

A chewy and crunchy combination
that's a piece of cake to make.

Chocolate-hazelnut Meringue Cake

1 tsp cornflour
1 tsp white wine vinegar
1 tsp vanilla extract
4 large egg whites
225g/8oz caster sugar
50g/2oz toasted hazelnuts, finely
chopped

TO FINISH
142ml carton double cream
100g bar dark chocolate, chopped
icing sugar, for dusting
cocoa powder, for dusting

Takes 1½ hours, plus cooling and
chilling • Cuts into 8 slices

1 Preheat oven to 140°C/Gas 1/fan oven
120°C. Line three baking sheets with
non-stick parchment, then draw three
20cm/8in circles on the paper.
2 Blend the cornflour to a paste with the
vinegar and vanilla. Whisk the egg whites to
stiff peaks, then gradually whisk in the sugar,
alternating with the paste until the meringue
is glossy. Fold in the nuts and spread over the
paper circles. Bake for 1 hour, turn off the
oven and leave the meringues inside for
another hour. Remove and set aside.
3 Scald the cream, add the chocolate and
stir until melted. Leave to cool for 1 hour
or until spreadable. If too runny, chill for
1 hour. Lift the meringues and sandwich
together with the filling. Chill until ready to
serve, then dust with icing sugar and cocoa.

• Per slice 301 kcalories, protein 4g, carbohydrate 36g,
fat 17g, saturated fat 8g, fibre 1g, sugar 35g,
salt 0.11g

Dust this cheesecake with cocoa powder, mark into portions and top
with chocolates for an impressive dessert for adults only!

Tia Maria Cheesecake

14 plain chocolate digestive biscuits,
finely crushed
85g/3oz butter, melted and hot
3 × 300g packs full-fat Philadelphia
cheese, at room temperature
200g/8oz golden caster sugar
4 tbsp plain flour
2 tsp vanilla extract
2 tbsp Tia Maria
3 large eggs, beaten
284ml carton soured cream

FOR THE TOPPING
142ml carton soured cream
2 tbsp Tia Maria
cocoa powder, for dusting
8 Ferrero Rocher chocolates

Takes 1 hour, plus cooling and chilling
• Cuts into 16 slices

1 Preheat oven to 180°C/Gas 4/fan oven
160°C. Line a 25cm/10in springform tin.
Blend the biscuit crumbs and butter, press
into the tin and bake for 10 minutes. Cool.
2 Turn oven up to 240°C/Gas 9/fan oven
200°C. Beat cheese and sugar until smooth,
then whisk in flour, vanilla, liqueur, eggs and
soured cream.
3 Butter the tin sides, then pour the mixture
in. Bake for 10 minutes, turn the oven down
to 110°C/Gas ¼/fan oven 90°C and bake for
another 25 minutes. Turn the oven off, open
the door and leave the cheesecake to cool
inside for 2 hours.
4 Mix the soured cream and liqueur together
then spread over the cheesecake. Chill.
To serve, remove from the tin and decorate.

• Per slice 410 kcalories, protein 7g, carbohydrate
32g, fat 29g, saturated fat 17g, fibre 1g, sugar 24g,
salt 0.89g

You could also serve this recipe as individual portions for a truly stunning dessert.

White Chocolate Mousse Cake

250g/9oz dark chocolate, chopped
75g/2½oz butter
3 tbsp coffee liqueur (e.g. Tia Maria or Kahlúa)
9 large eggs, separated
120g/4½oz caster sugar
175g/6oz ground almonds

FOR THE MOUSSE
150g/5oz white chocolate, chopped
600ml/1 pint double cream

TO SERVE
cocoa powder, for dusting
chocolate curls, to decorate

Takes 1½ hours, plus cooling and chilling • Cuts into 12 slices

1 Preheat oven to 180°C/Gas 4/fan oven 160°C. Oil and line a 25cm/10in tin. Melt the dark chocolate and butter with the liqueur in a bowl over a pan of hot water. Cool, then beat in the egg yolks and half the sugar.
2 Whisk the egg whites to stiff peaks and whisk in the remaining sugar. Gently fold into the chocolate mixture with the almonds. Pour into the tin and bake for 45–50 minutes until risen and a skewer comes out clean. Cool completely then remove from the tin.
3 For the mousse, melt the white chocolate in a bowl over a pan of hot water. Cool. Whip the cream until it holds its shape and fold in the melted chocolate. Place spoonfuls of the mousse over the cake and chill for at least 30 minutes. Serve dusted with cocoa powder and decorated with chocolate curls.

• Per slice 673 kcalories, protein 11.6g, carbohydrate 34.1g, fat 54.9g, saturated fat 25.9g, fibre 1.6g, sugar 33.6g, salt 0.33g

Delicious cup-cake drops of chocolate that are really easy to make and can be frozen ahead.

Chocolate Drop Cakes

150g pot natural yoghurt
3 eggs, beaten
1 tsp vanilla extract
175g (6oz) golden caster sugar
140g (5oz) self-raising flour (swap
1 tbsp of flour for cocoa powder)
100g (4oz) ground almonds
175g (6oz) unsalted butter, melted
chocolate buttons, to decorate

FOR THE CHOCOLATE FROSTING
100g (4oz) chocolate (milk or dark)
140g (5oz) unsalted butter
140g (5oz) icing sugar

Takes 18–20 minutes, plus icing •
Makes 12

1 Line a 12-hole muffin tin with paper cases and pre-heat oven to 190°C/Gas 5/fan oven 170°C. In a jug, mix the yoghurt, eggs and vanilla. Put the dry ingredients, plus a pinch of salt, into a large bowl and make a well in the middle. Add the yoghurty mix and melted butter, and quickly fold in – don't overwork it.
2 Spoon the mixture into the cases (they will be quite full) and bake for 18–20 mins or until golden, risen and springy to the touch. Cool for a few minutes, then lift the cakes on to a rack to cool completely.
3 To make the frosting, melt the chocolate in the microwave on High for 1½ mins, stirring halfway. Leave to cool. Beat the butter and icing sugar until creamy. Beat in the chocolate. Spread over the cakes and top with chocolate buttons. Keep cool.

• Per cake (with button) 492 kcalories, protein 6g, carbohydrate 47g, fat 32g, saturated fat 17g, fibre 1g, sugar 38g, salt 0.32g

If you want to get ahead, this trifle-like bombe can be made up to 2 days ahead or can be frozen for up to 3 months.

Mocha Almond Bombe

250g carton mascarpone, beaten until softened slightly
50g/2oz caster sugar
284ml carton double cream, whipped
100g/4oz dark chocolate, chopped
50g/2oz blanched almonds, toasted and roughly chopped
150ml/¼ pint cold strong black coffee
4 tbsp coffee liqueur (e.g. Tia Maria or Kahlúa)
1 large shop-bought Madeira cake, cut into 15 slices

TO SERVE
142ml carton double cream, whipped
icing sugar, for dusting

Takes 30 minutes, plus chilling •
Serves 6–8

1 Line a 1.4 litre/2½ pint pudding basin with cling film, leaving an overhang. Beat the mascarpone and sugar, then fold in the cream.
2 Mix the chocolate and almonds; set 2 tablespoons aside. Mix the coffee and liqueur. Line the bottom of the basin with cake slices and moisten with a little coffee mixture. Spread 2 spoonfuls of mascarpone over the cake, then cover with one-third of the chocolate and almonds. Do two more layers and finish with a layer of Madeira, moistened with the remaining coffee. Cover with the overhanging cling film and chill for 4 hours.
3 Unwrap the top of the bombe, invert it on to a plate and peel off the film. Cover with the cream, sprinkle over the reserved chocolate and almonds and dust with icing sugar.

• Per serving 940 kcalories, protein 8g, carbohydrate 64g, fat 73g, saturated fat 42g, fibre 2g, added sugar 46g, salt 0.75g

These oozing, gooey puds won't wait to be served, so make sure you have the delicious fruity sauce ready.

Chocolate and Polenta Puddings

cocoa powder, for dusting
140g/5oz dark chocolate, chopped
140g/5oz butter, diced
85g/3oz caster sugar
3 large eggs
3 large egg yolks
25g/1oz fine polenta
1 rounded tbsp plain flour
icing sugar, for dusting
6 Cape gooseberries,
to decorate

FOR THE SAUCE
8 passion fruit, halved
25g/1oz caster sugar

Takes 1 hour • Serves 6

1 Make the sauce. Scoop the passion-fruit pulp into a pan, add the sugar and stir over a low heat until dissolved and the pulp has separated from the seeds. Sieve (reserving a few seeds for the sauce) and leave to cool.
2 Preheat oven to 180°C/Gas 4/fan oven 160°C. Generously butter six 175–200ml/ 6–7fl oz dariole moulds, dust very generously with cocoa and put in the fridge.
3 Melt the chocolate and butter, then cool. Put the sugar, eggs and egg yolks in a large bowl and beat for 5 minutes until pale. Gradually whisk in the chocolate mixture.
4 Mix the polenta and flour, fold into the chocolate mixture and half-fill the moulds. Bake for 12–14 minutes until firm. Loosen the sides and turn out. Dust with icing sugar and decorate with Cape gooseberries.

• Per serving 511 kcalories, protein 8.2g, carbohydrate 46.5g, fat 33.7g, saturated fat 18.2g, fibre 1.8g, sugar 39.5g, salt 0.51g

A delicious twist on an old favourite makes these coffee-flavoured profiteroles the perfect end to a special meal.

Mocha Profiteroles

85g/3oz unsalted butter, diced
100g/4oz plain flour, sifted with
a pinch of salt
3 large eggs, beaten

FOR THE FILLING
4 tbsp custard powder
6 tbsp golden caster sugar
600ml/1 pint milk
2 tbsp coffee essence
100g/4oz icing sugar, sifted
284ml double cream, softly whipped

FOR THE SAUCE
100g/4oz dark chocolate, chopped
50g/2oz butter, diced
50ml/2fl oz strong black coffee
1–2 tbsp coffee liqueur (e.g. Tia
Maria or Kahlúa)

Takes 1¼ hours, plus cooling •
Serves 6

1 Make the choux buns. Bring the butter and 200ml/7fl oz water to the boil, remove from the heat and tip in the flour. Stir to form a paste, beat until it comes away from the pan, then tip out and leave to cool.
2 Preheat oven to 200°C/Gas 6/fan oven 180°C. Return the paste to the pan, then gradually beat in the eggs. Spoon walnut-sized balls on to a baking sheet and bake for 20–25 minutes until golden. Split the bottom of each bun with a teaspoon and bake upside-down for 5 minutes. Cool on a rack.
3 Make a thick custard with the powder, caster sugar and milk. Stir in the coffee and cool. Mix the icing sugar and cream, then fold into the custard and pipe into the buns.
4 Melt the chocolate, butter and coffee. Add the liqueur and pour over the buns.

• Per serving 807 kcalories, protein 11g, carbohydrate 73g, fat 54g, saturated fat 31g, fibre 1g, sugar 51g, salt 0.63g

For a lighter end to the Christmas dinner, try these zesty puddings, which can be frozen then thawed an hour before needed.

Iced Christmas Puddings

finely grated zest of 1 clementine
and 3 tbsp juice
5 tbsp dark rum or orange juice
140g/5oz golden caster sugar
85g/3oz mixed dried cranberries
and raisins
25g/1oz cut mixed peel
142ml carton double cream,
softly whipped
2 × 150g cartons light Greek
yoghurt, beaten until smooth
50g/2oz white chocolate, melted

Takes 30 minutes, plus cooling and
freezing • Serves 4

1 Line four 200ml/7fl oz moulds with cling film; leave an overhang. Heat the clementine juice with the rum and sugar until it dissolves. Add the dried fruit and simmer for 2 minutes. Stir in the zest and peel and leave until cold.
2 Fold the cream into the yoghurt. Put 4 tbsp of the fruit syrup in a container and freeze. Stir the rest into the yoghurt mix and divide among the moulds. Cover with the cling film, wrap in foil and freeze for up to a month.
3 Line a baking sheet with non-stick parchment. Draw 4 stars on the paper, turn it over, then trace them with drizzled chocolate. Leave to harden, then freeze in a container layered between greaseproof paper.
4 To serve, thaw fruit at room temperature, thaw puddings in the fridge. Top puddings with fruit, place the stars on the side.

• Per serving 494 kcalories, protein 6g, carbohydrate 60g, fat 23g, saturated fat 13g, fibre 1g, added sugar 39g, salt 0.22g

A delicious dessert that can be whipped up in under half an hour. Add a little kirsch or brandy to the cherry syrup for a boozy treat.

Black Forest Trifle

200g ready-made Madeira cake
425g can pitted black cherries in syrup
1 chocolate flake
100g packet plain chocolate drops
400g carton fresh custard
200ml carton crème fraîche

Takes 20 minutes, plus chilling • Serves 4 generously

1 Cut the cake into thick slices and use to line the base of a 2.5 litre/4½ pint serving bowl. Cut three cherries in half and reserve, and spoon the rest over the cake along with the syrup. Crumble half the flake over the cherries and scatter over half the chocolate drops.
2 Melt the remaining chocolate drops in a microwave-proof bowl on Medium for 2 minutes, stirring halfway through. Cool for 5 minutes, then whisk into the custard gradually, until you have a smooth chocolate custard. Pour over the cherries.
3 Spoon the crème fraîche over the custard. Sprinkle with the reserved cherries and crumble over the remaining flake. Chill until ready to serve.

• Per serving 478 kcalories, protein 7g, carbohydrate 59g, fat 25g, saturated fat 14g, fibre 1g, added sugar 16g, salt 0.57g

Soufflés always look impressive, so follow this simple recipe and wow your guests with this stunning pudding.

Dark Chocolate Soufflé

caster sugar, for dusting
140g/5oz dark chocolate, chopped
142ml carton double cream
½ tsp instant coffee powder
2 tbsp brandy
3 large eggs, separated
2 large egg whites
85g/3oz caster sugar
icing sugar, for dusting

FOR THE SAUCE
100g/4oz white chocolate, chopped
284ml carton double cream
1 tbsp brandy

Takes 45 minutes • Serves 4

1 Preheat oven to 220°C/Gas 7/fan oven 200°C. Brush a 1.4 litre/2½ pint soufflé dish with melted butter and dust with caster sugar.
2 In a small pan over a very low heat, melt the chocolate, cream and coffee until smooth. Remove from the heat and beat in the brandy and egg yolks. Cool slightly.
3 Whisk the egg whites until stiff. Add the caster sugar and whisk until glossy. Fold a quarter into the chocolate, fold it back into the remaining whites, then spoon into the dish. Run a knife around the inside at the top of the dish (to help even rising), then bake for 20–25 minutes until well risen and just firm.
4 Make the sauce. Gently melt the chocolate and cream in a pan then stir in the brandy. Serve with the soufflé dusted with icing sugar.

• Per serving 982 kcalories, protein 12g, carbohydrate 63g, fat 75g, saturated fat 40g, fibre 1g, added sugar 57g, salt 0.44g

A sensational, summery cheesecake that requires no cooking. Prepare ahead and simply drizzle with blueberry sauce on the day.

White Chocolate Cheesecake

100g/4oz plain digestive biscuits
50g/2oz butter, melted
400g/14oz white chocolate, broken into pieces
284ml carton double cream
250g/9oz full-fat soft cheese
250g carton mascarpone

FOR THE BLUEBERRY SAUCE
275g/10oz blueberries, plus extra to serve
50g/2oz caster sugar
1 tbsp lemon juice

Takes 30 minutes, plus 5 minutes chilling • Serves 10

1 Whiz biscuits to crumbs in a food processor, add the butter and pulse. Base-line a 20cm/8in springform cake tin with non-stick baking parchment. Cover base evenly with mixture. Cover and chill.
2 For topping, put chocolate in a heatproof bowl over a pan of simmering water. Remove from the heat and set aside until melted. Stir, remove from pan and leave to cool slightly.
3 Beat the cream, cheese and mascarpone in a bowl and stir in the chocolate. Spoon over base and chill for 3 hours.
4 Tip half the blueberries into a blender with the sugar and lemon juice. Blend until smooth. Press through a sieve and set aside.
5 Remove the cheesecake from tin and slice. Drizzle over sauce and top with blueberries.

• Per serving 802 kcalories, protein 9g, carbohydrate 49g, fat 65g, saturated fat 24g, fibre 1g, added sugar 32g, salt 0.83g

Light up Bonfire Night with your own sparkling dinner-table display.
Serve it up with hot chocolate sauce as the last spark dies.

Chocolate Bombe Alaska

20cm shop-bought chocolate
sponge cake
grated zest of 1 orange
5 tbsp marmalade
2 × 600ml tubs vanilla ice cream,
softened in the fridge for
30 minutes
400ml/14fl oz orange sorbet,
softened slightly
hot chocolate sauce, to serve

FOR THE MERINGUE TOPPING
4 large egg whites
225g/8oz caster sugar

Takes 1 hour, plus freezing • Serves 8

1 Line a 1 litre/1¾ pint pudding basin with cling film, leave an overhang. Cut a cake circle for the bottom and triangular pieces for the sides, fill gaps with trimmings. Freeze.
2 Beat the orange zest and marmalade into the ice cream. Scoop into the cake-lined basin, and make an indent by sitting a small bowl in the top. Freeze for 1 hour, or until just firm, then fill the indent with sorbet. Cover the top with sponge, then with the surplus cling film. Freeze for at least 8 hours.
3 To serve, preheat oven to 230°C/Gas 8/ fan oven 210°C. Whisk the egg whites to stiff peaks, then gradually whisk in the sugar. Turn the bombe on to an ovenproof dish, remove the film and swirl the meringue all over to make a complete seal. Bake for 10–15 minutes or until golden.

• Per serving 505 kcalories, protein 7.5g, carbohydrate 83.7g, fat 17.9g, saturated fat 9.5g, fibre 0.7g, sugar 73.5g, salt 0.61g

A delicious dessert for a special dinner at home or after a day on the piste.

Mini Monts Blancs

5 large egg whites
300g/10oz caster sugar
2 tsp cornflour blended with 1 tsp white wine vinegar
100g/4oz dark chocolate
250g can sweetened chestnut purée
2 tbsp dark rum (optional)
250ml/9fl oz double cream
grated chocolate, to serve

Takes 1½ hours, plus cooling and chilling • Serves 8

1 Preheat oven to 140°C/Gas 1/fan oven 120°C. Line two baking sheets with non-stick parchment. Whisk the egg whites until stiff. Gradually whisk in the sugar until glossy. Whisk in cornflour mixture. Spoon eight 10cm/4in meringue mounds on to the baking sheets, peaking in the centre. Bake for 50–60 minutes until crisp. Cool on a rack.
2 Chop and melt 85g/3oz of the chocolate. Put the chestnut purée in a bowl and stir in the rum (if using) then the melted chocolate. Whip half the cream to soft peaks and stir into the chestnut mixture. Chill until firm.
3 Spoon the chestnut mixture on top of the meringues, swirling to a peak. Whip the remaining cream to soft peaks and spoon on top to resemble snow caps. Chill for up to 2 hours, then serve with grated chocolate.

• Per serving 423 kcalories, protein 4g, carbohydrate 63g, fat 19g, saturated fat 12g, fibre 2g, added sugar 50g, salt 0.14g

A temptingly gooey and rich chocolate cake. Serve with cream and fresh blueberries to lighten the palette.

Dorset Chocolate Mousse Cake

350g/12oz dark chocolate (about 70% solids), chopped
225g/8oz unsalted butter, diced
5 large organic eggs
300g/10oz golden caster sugar
100g/4oz butter biscuits or shortbread, broken into bite-sized pieces

TO SERVE
284ml carton double cream
225g/8oz blueberries

Takes 1–1¼ hours, plus cooling and optional chilling • Serves 8

1 Preheat oven to 160°C/Gas 3/fan oven 140°C. Butter and line a 23cm/9½in springform cake tin. Melt the chocolate and butter together. Using an electric mixer, beat the eggs with the sugar for about 5 minutes until the mixture is thick and pale and has doubled in volume.
2 Pour the chocolate into the whisked egg mixture and fold in gently but thoroughly. Add the broken biscuits and gently fold again.
3 Pour the mixture into the tin and bake for 40–45 minutes until just firm. Allow to cool in the tin for ½–¾ hour before serving warm and gooey (as in the picture), or chill for up to 24 hours until firm and fudgy enough to cut into wedges. Serve with cream and fresh blueberries.

• Per serving 720 kcalories, protein 9g, carbohydrate 67g, fat 48g, saturated fat 27g, fibre 3g, added sugar 52g, salt 0.22g

Served with a pile of berried fruits and thick cream, this pudding is perfect for a warm summer's evening.

Chocolate Tart with Raspberries

FOR THE PASTRY
100g/4oz plain flour
50g/2oz ground almonds
85g/3oz butter, diced
25g/1oz golden caster sugar
1 large egg yolk

FOR THE FILLING
2 large egg whites
100g/4oz golden caster sugar
150g bar dark chocolate, melted
142ml carton double cream, whipped to a soft peak
2 tbsp brandy

TO SERVE
284ml carton double cream, whipped
450g/1lb raspberries and blueberries
icing sugar, for dusting

Takes 1½ hours, plus chilling and cooling • Serves 6–8

1 Work the flour, almonds and butter into crumbs in a food processor. Mix to a dough with the sugar, egg yolk and 1 tablespoon cold water. Knead briefly, wrap in cling film and chill for 15–20 minutes.

2 Preheat oven to 190°C/Gas 5/fan oven 170°C. Roll out the dough and use to line a 24cm/9½in flan tin. Bake blind with foil and beans for 15 minutes, then remove foil and beans and bake 7–10 minutes more until crisp and golden. Cool.

3 For the filling, whisk the egg whites and sugar in a bowl over a pan of simmering water for 5 minutes until thick and glossy. Remove from the heat, whisk for 2 minutes. Fold in the chocolate, cream and brandy, pour into the pastry case and chill until set.

• Per serving for 6 794 kcalories, protein 8g, carbohydrate 59g, fat 59g, saturated fat 34g, fibre 3g, added sugar 39g, salt 0.42g

A spectacular summer trifle. If you're entertaining people who can't eat raw egg, or you want a lighter pudding, leave out the eggs.

Choco-berry Trifle

600g/1lb 5oz strawberries, hulled and roughly sliced
4 tbsp orange juice
500g carton mascarpone
100g/4oz golden caster sugar
3 large eggs, separated
8 ready-made chocolate brownies
50g/2oz dark chocolate, grated or shaved into curls

Takes 25–35 minutes, plus soaking and chilling • Serves 8

This mousse contains raw egg whites, which should be avoided by those in vulnerable groups.

1 Mix the strawberries with the orange juice in a large bowl. Soak for about 30 minutes.
2 Beat the mascarpone with the sugar and egg yolks until smooth. Whisk the egg whites to soft peaks, then gently stir a little into the mascarpone mixture to lighten it. Gently fold in the rest.
3 Halve the brownies horizontally. Tuck half of them snugly into the bottom of a glass trifle bowl (you may need to cut them to fit). Add half the strawberry mixture and juices, then half the mascarpone mixture. Top with another layer of brownies, then with the remaining strawberry mixture and juices. Finally, spread the remaining mascarpone on top. Cover and chill for several hours or overnight.
4 To serve, scatter with grated chocolate or chocolate curls.

• Per serving 590 kcalories, protein 7g, carbohydrate 48g, fat 42g, saturated fat 24g, fibre 2g, added sugar 29g, salt 0.42g

A quick and easy dessert that you can store in the freezer
for up to a month.

Smooth Chocolate Sorbet

225g/8oz caster sugar
200g/7oz dark chocolate

Takes 15–20 minutes, plus cooling,
chilling and freezing • Serves 4

1 First make a sugar syrup. Tip the sugar into a heavy pan, pour in 500ml/18fl oz water and boil until the sugar has dissolved. Remove from the heat and cool completely.
2 While the syrup is cooling, chop the chocolate and melt in a bowl over a pan of hot water (or in the microwave on High), then leave to cool completely.
3 When both the syrup and the melted chocolate are cool (this is very important), slowly combine the two in a large bowl. Place the bowl in the fridge until the mix is well chilled, then churn in an ice-cream machine. Once the sorbet is frozen, decant into a freezer container and store in the freezer.

• Per serving 477 kcalories, protein 2.5g, carbohydrate 90.8g, fat 14g, saturated fat 8g, fibre 1.3g, sugar 90.4g, salt 0.01g

A popular favourite when served in cups becomes a smart finale for a dinner party, particularly presented with elegant, crisp biscuits.

Chocolate Mousse

200g bar dark chocolate
2 tbsp brandy
3 large organic egg whites
50g/2oz golden caster sugar
100ml/3½ fl oz whipping cream,
whipped to a soft peak

TO SERVE
icing sugar, for dusting
crisp biscuits, such as
langues-de-chat

Takes 20–30 minutes, plus chilling •
Serves 6

This mousse contains raw egg whites,
which should be avoided by those in
vulnerable groups.

1 Chop 150g/5oz of the chocolate and melt in a bowl over a pan of hot water. Take the pan off the heat, but keep the bowl over the water and stir in the brandy. Grate the remaining chocolate and set aside.
2 Whisk the egg whites to stiff peaks. Whisk in the sugar a spoonful at a time to make a glossy meringue. Take the chocolate off the pan and fold in a heaped tablespoon of meringue, then tip the chocolate into the meringue and fold in lightly but thoroughly. Now fold in the cream and two-thirds of the grated chocolate. Divide among six small cups and chill for 2 hours, or overnight.
3 Serve sprinkled with the remaining grated chocolate and icing sugar, with the biscuits tucked alongside.

• Per serving 283 kcalories, protein 4g, carbohydrate 30g, fat 16g, saturated fat 9g, fibre 1g, added sugar 30g, salt 0.11g

Cherries and chocolate are a winning combination, and this cherry-choc terrine makes the perfect end to a special meal.

Cherry-choc Terrine

225g/8oz dark chocolate (50–70% cocoa solids), chopped
150g/5oz unsalted butter, diced and softened
100g/4oz golden caster sugar
25g/1oz cocoa powder
284ml carton double cream
3 medium organic egg whites
125ml/4fl oz cherry liqueur or brandy
280g/10oz cherries (fresh or canned), pitted

TO SERVE
125ml/4fl oz cherry liqueur or brandy
50g/2oz golden caster sugar
500g carton mascarpone

Takes 1–1¼ hours, plus cooling and freezing • Serves 10

1 Line a 1.7 litre/3 pint loaf tin with cling film, leaving an overhang. Melt the chocolate with half the butter; cool. Cream the remaining butter with the sugar and cocoa.
2 Whip the cream to soft peaks. In another bowl, whisk the egg whites to soft peaks.
3 Stir the liqueur into the cocoa mix, then stir in the melted chocolate and the cherries. Fold in the cream, then the egg whites until evenly mixed. Pour into the tin and gently tap the bottom to settle the mixture. Wrap and freeze overnight, or for up to a month.
4 To serve, boil the liqueur and sugar in a small, heavy pan until reduced to a syrup. Cool. Unmould the terrine, remove the film and leave for 10–15 minutes. Slice and arrange on plates with a dollop of mascarpone, then drizzle with the syrup.

• Per serving 771 kcalories, protein 4.8g, carbohydrate 39.6g, fat 60.8g, saturated fat 35.9g, fibre 1.9g, sugar 34.4g, salt 0.21g

Use frozen berries and you can enjoy a taste of summer all year round with this spectacular semifreddo.

Semifreddo with Chocolate Sauce

3 large egg whites
1 tsp instant coffee powder, dissolved in boiling water, cooled
175g/6oz golden caster sugar
50g/2oz toasted chopped hazelnuts
2 × 284ml cartons double cream, whipped to a soft peak
500g bag frozen mixed berries

FOR THE SAUCE
142ml carton double cream
1 tbsp golden syrup
3 tbsp water
140g/5oz dark chocolate (preferably 70% cocoa solids), chopped
25g/1oz butter

Takes 3½–3¾ hours, plus cooling, freezing and defrosting • Serves 6

1 Preheat oven to 110°C/Gas ¼/fan oven 90°C. Line a baking sheet with non-stick paper. Whisk egg whites with the coffee until stiff. Whisk in half the sugar, then the nuts and remaining sugar. Spread 2cm/¾in deep on paper and bake for 3 hours. Cool.
2 Line a loose-bottomed 20cm/8in cake tin. Break up the meringue, mix two-thirds into the cream and spread a third in the tin. Cover with half the berries. Repeat, then top with remaining cream and meringue. Cover with cling film and a plate. Wrap and freeze.
3 Transfer to fridge for 2–3 hours. Unwrap on to a plate, and return to fridge for 5 hours.
4 Heat the cream, syrup and water until bubbling. Add the chocolate and butter and melt, stirring. Pour sauce over the cake.

• Per serving 893 kcalories, protein 8g, carbohydrate 49g, fat 76g, saturated fat 44g, fibre 4g, added sugar 39g, salt 0.32g

Individual soufflés make an impressive finale when dusted with icing sugar or served with a scoop of vanilla ice cream.

Chocolate-orange Soufflés

25g/1oz ground almonds
175g pack Terry's plain chocolate orange, broken into segments
25g/1oz butter
4 large eggs, separated
icing sugar, for dusting

Takes 35 minutes • Serves 6

1 Preheat oven to 190°C/Gas 5/fan oven 170°C. Butter six 125ml/4fl oz ramekins and dust with the ground almonds.
2 Set aside three chocolate segments. Break the remaining chocolate into a bowl, add the butter. Set the bowl over a pan of hot water. When the chocolate has melted, lift the bowl off and set aside to cool for 5 minutes. Stir in the egg yolks.
3 Whisk the egg whites in a separate bowl until stiff. Stir a quarter of the egg whites into the chocolate mix, then carefully fold in the remaining egg whites with a metal spoon.
4 Divide the mixture among the dishes. Tuck half a chocolate segment into the centre of each dish. Bake for about 10 minutes until risen. Serve immediately.

• Per soufflé 245 kcalories, protein 6g, carbohydrate 21g, fat 16g, saturated fat 6g, fibre 1g, added sugar 18g, salt 0.27g

The perfect pudding to end a relaxed, autumnal Sunday lunch – so leave plenty of room for it!

Prune and Chocolate Torte

250g/9 oz no-soak prunes, halved
4 tbsp brandy
25g/1oz cocoa powder
100g/4oz dark chocolate (at least 70% cocoa solids), broken into pieces
50g/2oz butter, diced
175g/6oz caster sugar
4 large egg whites
85g/3oz plain flour
1 tsp ground cinnamon
lightly whipped cream or crème fraîche, to serve

Takes 1 hour 5 minutes, plus 30 minutes soaking • Serves 8

1 Soak the prunes in brandy for about 30 minutes. Preheat the oven to 190°C/ Gas 5/fan oven 170°C. Butter a 23cm/9in loose-bottomed cake tin. Put the cocoa, chocolate, butter and 140g/5oz of the sugar in a pan, add 100ml/3½ fl oz hot water and gently heat until smooth. Leave to cool.
2 Whisk the egg whites to soft peaks, then gradually whisk in the remaining sugar. Sift the flour and cinnamon over and gently fold in with a metal spoon, until almost combined. Add the chocolate mixture and fold in until evenly combined.
3 Pour the mixture into the tin and arrange the prunes over the top. Sprinkle over any remaining brandy and bake for about 30 minutes until just firm. Serve with cream or crème fraîche.

• Per serving 311 kcalories, protein 5g, carbohydrate 51g, fat 10g, saturated fat 6g, fibre 3g, added sugar 31g, salt 0.18g

A spectacular dessert that looks impressive
but is deceptively easy to make.

Kahlúa Chocolate Cheesecake

50g/2oz butter
225g/8oz plain chocolate digestive biscuits, crushed
225g/8oz dark chocolate (at least 50% cocoa solids), chopped
2 × 200g packs full-fat soft cheese, at room temperature
100g/4oz golden caster sugar
4 medium eggs
284ml carton double cream
5 tbsp Kahlúa (coffee liqueur)

FOR THE TOPPING
200ml carton crème fraîche
2 tbsp Kahlúa, plus extra to serve
cocoa powder, for dusting

Takes 1½ hours, plus cooling and chilling • Serves 12

1 Melt the butter in a pan, stir in the crushed biscuits and press over the bottom of a lightly oiled 23cm/9in cake tin. Chill.
2 Melt the chocolate in a bowl over a pan of hot water then remove. Preheat oven to 160°C/Gas 3/fan oven 140°C.
3 Beat the cheese and sugar until fluffy. Add the eggs one at a time; don't overbeat. Slowly blend in the chocolate, cream and liqueur. Pour over the biscuit base and bake for 55–60 minutes until set. The top should be shiny and wobbly and dark in the centre. Loosen the cheesecake around the tin and cool. Chill for 3 hours or overnight.
4 Remove the cheesecake from the tin. Combine the crème fraîche and Kahlúa and spread over the top. Serve dusted with cocoa and sprinkled with Kahlúa.

• Per serving 583 kcalories, protein 7.5g, carbohydrate 34.3g, fat 45.1g, saturated fat 25.4g, fibre 1.7g, sugar 23.4g, salt 0.71g

If you've never made a soufflé before in your life, with this can't-fail recipe you're guaranteed to impress yourself and your guests.

Hot Chocolate Soufflés

2 tbsp ground almonds
150g bar dark chocolate, chopped
4 tbsp strong black coffee, or coffee or hazelnut liqueur
2 tsp plain flour
100g/4oz caster sugar
4 large eggs, separated
vanilla ice cream, to serve

FOR THE SAUCE
142ml carton double cream
100g/4oz dark chocolate, chopped
2 tbsp strong black coffee, or coffee or hazelnut liqueur

Takes 1 hour • Serves 6

1 Preheat oven to 190°C/Gas 5/fan oven 170°C. Generously butter six 200ml/7fl oz ramekins and dust with the almonds.
2 Melt the chocolate with the coffee and cool. Stir in the flour, half the sugar and the egg yolks. Whisk the egg whites until stiff, gradually adding the remaining sugar. Fold into the chocolate mixture and pour into the ramekins. (The soufflés can now be covered with foil and set aside for up to an hour.)
3 Bake for 15–20 minutes until risen with a firm crust. Make the sauce by scalding the cream in a pan. Remove from the heat and add the chocolate. Stir until the sauce is smooth and glossy, then stir in the coffee.
4 To serve, split the top of each soufflé and add a small scoop of ice cream followed by a drizzle of sauce.

• Per soufflé 503 kcalories, protein 10g, carbohydrate 39g, fat 35g, saturated fat 17g, fibre 3g, added sugar 28g, salt 0.17g

If you can't get strawberries for this dessert, try another seasonal berry, or use peach or nectarine slices.

Chocolate Pavlova

2 tsp cornflour
2 tsp white vinegar
2 tsp vanilla extract
5 large egg whites
300g/10oz caster sugar
50g/2oz dark chocolate (50–70% cocoa solids), grated
1 tbsp cocoa powder, sifted, plus extra for dusting

TO FINISH
425ml/¾ pint double cream, whipped
450g/1lb strawberries, hulled and halved (leave a few whole)
25g/1oz toasted hazelnuts

Takes 1½ hours, plus cooling • Serves 6

1 Preheat oven to 140°C/Gas 1/fan oven 120°C. Line a baking sheet with non-stick parchment. Blend the cornflour, vinegar and vanilla to a paste.
2 Whisk the egg whites until stiff, gradually whisk in the sugar and add the cornflour paste until you have a thick, heavy mixture. Put half the mixture in a bowl and stir in the chocolate and cocoa. Fold together, then spoon back into the meringue, swirling briefly.
3 Spoon on to the paper to make a 23cm/9in disc with a dip in the centre. Dust cocoa around the edge; swirl with a skewer to form peaks. Bake for 1 hour, turn off oven and leave inside for 1 hour. Remove, cool.
4 Pile the cream on the meringue. Pile the strawberries on top and sprinkle with nuts.

• Per serving 631 kcalories, protein 5g, carbohydrate 68g, fat 40g, saturated fat 23g, fibre 2g, added sugar 59g, salt 0.26g

A tempting teatime treat here becomes a divinely elegant dinner-party dessert.

Brownie Pudding

140g/5oz dark chocolate, chopped
175g/6oz butter, diced
175g/6oz light muscovado sugar
225g/8oz self-raising flour
1 tbsp cocoa powder
2 large eggs, beaten
100g/4oz walnuts, roughly chopped

TO SERVE
100g/4oz white chocolate, chopped
284ml carton double cream

Takes 2¼ hours • Serves 6–8

1 Butter and line a 1.7 litre/3 pint pudding basin. In a bowl over a pan of hot water, stir the dark chocolate, butter, sugar and 200ml/7fl oz water, to make a smooth sauce. Remove the bowl and cool for 10 minutes.
2 Sift the flour and cocoa into a bowl, then fold into the chocolate mixture with the eggs and nuts. Stir gently until well mixed, spoon into the pudding basin and smooth the top. Cover with a double thickness of pleated greaseproof paper and tie with string. Overwrap with foil, tucking in the ends, and steam in a covered pan of simmering water for 1½–1¾ hours until risen and firm.
3 Melt the white chocolate with the cream, stirring to make a smooth sauce. Invert the pudding on a plate and serve with the sauce.

• Per serving for 8 774 kcalories, protein 8.6g, carbohydrate 61.2g, fat 56.7g, saturated fat 28.7g, fibre 1.8g, sugar 41.9g, salt 0.70g

Steeped in brandy, Tia Maria and coffee, this is your dessert,
coffee and liqueur courses all in one!

Boozy Chocolate Gâteau

250g carton mascarpone
284ml carton double cream
25g/1oz icing sugar
3 tbsp instant coffee powder
dissolved in 85ml/3fl oz boiling
water, cooled
1 tbsp caster sugar
2 tbsp brandy
14 sponge fingers
85g/3oz dark chocolate, chopped
into very small pieces
2 tbsp dark rum
12 amaretti biscuit halves
2 tbsp Tia Maria
25g/1oz flaked almonds, toasted,
to decorate

Takes 40 minutes, plus chilling •
Serves 8

1 Whisk the mascarpone, cream and icing sugar with 50ml/2fl oz of the coffee. Chill. Heat the caster sugar with the remaining coffee until dissolved. Cool.
2 Divide the coffee syrup into three. Add brandy to one third in a shallow dish and dip in 7 sponge fingers. Lay them in a line on a plate, touching. Cover with a third of the coffee cream, then sprinkle with a third of the chocolate. Mix a third of the syrup with the rum, dip in the amaretti and arrange over the chocolate. Cover with the next layer of coffee cream, sprinkle with a third of the chocolate.
3 Mix the remaining syrup with the Tia Maria, dip in more sponge fingers and lay in a line on the chocolate. Cover with the last coffee cream and chill for 24 hours. Serve decorated with almonds and chocolate.

• Per serving 674 kcalories, protein 6g, carbohydrate 49g, fat 48g, saturated fat 26g, fibre 1g, added sugar 31g, salt 0.7g

*An irresistible combination of crunchy meringue
and smooth custard.*

Chocolate Îles Flottantes

600ml/1 pint milk
1 vanilla pod, split lengthways and
seeds scraped out
6 large egg yolks
100g/4oz caster sugar
coarsely grated dark chocolate,
to serve

FOR THE MERINGUES
2 large egg whites
50g/2oz caster sugar
1 tbsp cocoa powder, sifted

Takes 50–60 minutes, plus cooling and
optional chilling • Serves 6

1 Warm the milk, vanilla pod and seeds in a non-stick pan over a low heat for 5 minutes. Whisk the egg yolks and sugar until pale and thick, then gradually whisk in the milk. Return to the pan and stir over a low heat for about 10 minutes until the custard lightly coats the back of a wooden spoon. Strain into a bowl, cover with cling film, and leave to cool.
2 Whisk the egg whites to stiff peaks, adding the sugar in three batches. Whisk in the cocoa. Divide among six tea cups and microwave on High, one at a time, for 10–15 seconds until firm to the touch. Cool.
3 Divide the custard among six glasses. Invert each meringue into your hand, then slide on top of a custard. Serve immediately, or chill for up to an hour. Sprinkle with chocolate before serving.

• Per serving 232 kcalories, protein 8.1g, carbohydrate 31.8g, fat 8.9g, saturated fat 3.1g, fibre 0.2g, sugar 31.2g, salt 0.21g

An incredibly quick, virtually no-cook treat that you can make in the morning and enjoy for afternoon tea.

Chocolate and Nut Cake

400g/14oz dark chocolate, chopped
100g/4oz butter, diced
50g/2oz caster sugar
½ tsp ground cinnamon
225g/8oz macaroons or coconut
biscuits, broken into pieces
100g/4oz Brazil nuts, roughly
chopped
desiccated coconut, for sprinkling

Takes 20 minutes, plus chilling •
Cuts into 6 slices

1 Line a 900g/2lb loaf tin with a double layer of cling film, leaving an overhang. Melt the chocolate, butter and sugar in a bowl over a pan of hot water (or in the microwave on Medium for 2–3 minutes). Remove the bowl and stir in the cinnamon, macaroons and nuts.
2 Pour the mixture into the tin, smooth the surface and cover with the surplus cling film. Leave the cake to set in the fridge for at least 2 hours.
3 To serve, unwrap the cling film from the top of the cake and turn the cake out of the tin on to a plate. Remove the cling film and sprinkle the cake with desiccated coconut.

• Per slice 759 kcalories, protein 9g, carbohydrate 73g, fat 50g, saturated fat 22g, fibre 3g, added sugar 70g, salt 0.32g

The perfect lightning-fast and enticingly summery dessert that's ideal for an impromptu dinner at any time of year.

Chocolate Iced Berries

500g/1lb 2oz mixed frozen berries (blackberries, blueberries, raspberries, redcurrants)

FOR THE SAUCE
142ml carton double cream
140g/5oz white chocolate
1 tbsp white rum (optional)

Takes 15 minutes • Serves 4

1 Make the sauce. Pour the cream into a small pan and break in the chocolate. Heat gently, stirring, until the chocolate melts into a smooth sauce. Take care not to overheat or the chocolate will seize into a hard lump. Remove from the heat and stir in the rum (if using).
2 Scatter the frozen berries over four dessert plates or in shallow bowls. Pour the hot chocolate sauce over the fruits and serve immediately. The heat of the hot sauce will make the fruits start to defrost and become juicy.

• Per serving 377 kcalories, protein 5g, carbohydrate 28g, fat 28g, saturated fat 11g, fibre 3g, added sugar 17g, salt 0.14g

This no-cook dessert uses ready-made ingredients,
so it's the perfect pudding when time is tight.

Banoffee trifles

6 tbsp tropical fruit juice (from a carton)
2 tbsp dark rum or brandy
2 firm bananas, peeled and sliced
8 thin slices shop-bought Madeira cake
2 tbsp good-quality chocolate sauce
4 heaped tbsp dulce de leche (banoffee toffee)
250g carton mascarpone
250ml/9fl oz chilled ready-made custard
a block of dark chocolate (any size will do), to serve

Takes 20 minutes, plus chilling • Serves 4

1 Mix the fruit juice and alcohol in a large bowl. Toss in the bananas. Sandwich the slices of Madeira cake with the chocolate sauce, dice into squares and pile in the bottom of four glasses. Top with the banana mixture, then add a heaped tablespoonful of dulce de leche to make another layer.
2 Beat the mascarpone and custard together until smooth, then spoon on top of the puddings. Chill until ready to serve, for up to 2 hours.
3 Before serving, run a vegetable peeler down the flat back of the block of chocolate to make shavings. Scatter the shavings indulgently on top of the trifles.

• Per serving 714 kcalories, protein 8.5g, carbohydrate 75g, fat 42.7g, saturated fat 25.1g, fibre 1.1g, sugar 58.5g, salt 0.84g

This speedy, light, frothy mousse is most tempting when made with high-quality dark chocolate.

Cappuccino Mousse

125g/4½oz dark chocolate
1 tbsp instant coffee granules
2 tbsp Tia Maria (coffee liqueur)
4 medium egg whites
140g/5oz caster sugar
300ml/½ pint double cream
cocoa powder, to dust

Takes 15 minutes, plus chilling •
Serves 6

1 Melt the chocolate in a bowl set over a pan of simmering water, making sure the bowl doesn't touch the water. Remove from the heat and cool. Dissolve the coffee in two tablespoons of boiling water and stir in the Tia Maria. Stir into the chocolate.
2 In a bowl whisk the egg whites to soft peaks. Gradually whisk in the caster sugar until thick. Stir two tablespoons of the meringue into the chocolate mixture to slacken it and then fold in the remainder. Spoon the mousse into six cappuccino cups and chill for at least 20 minutes.
3 Lightly whip the cream and spoon over the mousses. Dust with cocoa to serve.

• Per serving 461 kcalories, protein 5g, carbohydrate 42g, fat 31g, saturated fat 19g, fibre 0.5g, added sugar 38g, salt 0.22g

A yummy teatime treat for hungry home-coming schoolchildren, and with minimal cooking involved, they can help you make it.

Blueberry Rocky-Road Squares

200g/7oz dark chocolate, chopped
200g/7oz (half a can) condensed milk
25g/1oz butter
100g/4oz Brazil nuts
75g pack dried blueberries
200g pack mini marshmallows
50g/2oz white chocolate, chopped

Takes 20 minutes, plus chilling • Makes 16

1 Line a 23cm/9in square cake tin with non-stick parchment. Melt the dark chocolate, milk and butter in a large bowl over a pan of hot water (or microwave on High for 1–1½ minutes). Beat until smooth. Stir in the nuts, blueberries and marshmallows. Pour into the tin and spread evenly.

2 Melt the white chocolate in a bowl over a pan of hot water (or in the microwave on High for 30–60 seconds). Give the chocolate a quick stir, then drizzle over the top of the mixture. Chill for at least 30 minutes until set. Cut into squares to serve.

• Per square 199 kcalories, protein 3g, carbohydrate 24g, fat 11g, saturated fat 5g, fibre 1g, sugar 16g, salt 0.1g

The easiest dessert for adults and children alike. You don't have to use raspberries, just any fruit you have to hand.

Raspberry and Snickers Ice Cream

1.5 litres/2¾ pints vanilla ice cream
2 Snickers bars
300g/10oz raspberries
single cream, to serve (optional)

Takes 10 minutes, plus freezing • Serves 6

1 Put the ice cream in the microwave on Defrost for 4–5 minutes to soften. Chop the Snickers bars into small pieces. Mash half the raspberries.

2 Tip the ice cream into a bowl. Fold in the mashed raspberries and three-quarters of the Snickers. Pack into a rigid container and freeze until firm.

3 To serve, scoop the ice cream on to serving plates and scatter with the remaining raspberries and Snickers. Drizzle over a little single cream if you like.

• Per serving 570 kcalories, protein 11g, carbohydrate 73g, fat 28g, saturated fat 18g, fibre 1g, added sugar 46g, salt 0.55g

A truly indulgent take on the traditional fondue,
and an ideal way to end an informal meal.

White Chocolate Fondue

200g/7oz white chocolate, chopped
50g/2oz unsalted butter, diced
142ml carton double cream
1 tsp vanilla extract
250g/9oz cherries or blackberries, chilled
250g/9oz strawberries, chilled

Takes 15 minutes • Serves 4

1 Combine the chocolate, butter, cream and vanilla in a bowl over a pan of hot water. Heat for about 5 minutes until melted and smooth, stirring occasionally.
2 Transfer to a fondue pot or warm pan, and serve with the chilled cherries or blackberries and the strawberries for dipping.

• Per serving 577 kcalories, protein 6g, carbohydrate 40g, fat 45g, saturated fat 26g, fibre 1g, added sugar 24g, salt 0.17g

A mouth-watering muffin in minutes and a chocolatey treat that will fast become a family favourite.

Choco-mel Muffins

50g chocolate caramel bar, chopped
2 tbsp double cream
2 ready-made chocolate muffins
2 scoops vanilla ice cream

Takes 15 minutes • Makes 2

1 Put the pieces of chocolate caramel bar and the cream in a heavy pan and place over a low heat until melted and smooth, stirring all the time. Remove from the heat.
2 Scoop a little cake from the middle of each muffin to make a hollow, then top each one with a scoop of ice cream. Drizzle with the caramel sauce and serve immediately.

• Per muffin 486 kcalories, protein 6.7g, carbohydrate 52.3g, fat 29.3g, saturated fat 16.1g, fibre 0.6g, added sugar 38.8g, salt 0.43g

Turn digestive biscuits into a zesty treat that can be served warm or chilled.

Chocolate Cheesecake Cups

50g/2oz milk or dark chocolate, chopped
finely grated zest and chopped flesh of 2 oranges
4 tbsp icing sugar
200g pack light soft cheese (e.g. Philadelphia Light)
4 digestive biscuits, roughly crushed

Takes 20 minutes, plus optional chilling • Serves 4

1 Melt the chocolate in a bowl over a pan of hot water (or in the microwave on High for 2 minutes), stirring halfway. Stir in half the orange zest and set aside.

2 Beat the sugar into the cheese, then fold in the orange pieces. Divide the crushed biscuits among four glasses or teacups, spoon over the cheese mix and serve with a drizzle of chocolate sauce. Sprinkle over the remaining zest. Eat straightaway, or chill for a crisp topping.

• Per serving 314 kcalories, protein 7g, carbohydrate 44g, fat 13g, saturated fat 7g, fibre 2g, sugar 35g, salt 0.81g

A fantastic cheat's recipe that needs no cooking and uses ready-made cakes and custard, but will taste as good as it looks.

Peach and Chocolate Trifle

142ml carton whipping cream
500g carton custard
zest and juice of 1 large orange
4 tbsp Cointreau
1 shop-bought Madeira cake
6 peaches or nectarines, stoned and thinly sliced
50g/2oz dark chocolate, coarsely grated
icing sugar, for dusting

Takes 30 minutes, plus optional chilling • Serves 6

1 Whip the cream until stiff, then fold into the custard. Grate the orange zest and stir into the custard. Squeeze the orange juice, and mix with the Cointreau.

2 Cut the cake into cubes, place in a glass bowl and sprinkle with the orange juice mixture. Scatter half the fruit slices over the cake, then sprinkle the grated chocolate on top. Spoon over the custard. Arrange the remaining fruit slices on top and dust with icing sugar. Serve straightaway, or cover and chill until ready to serve.

• Per serving 571 kcalories, protein 8g, carbohydrate 66g, fat 24g, saturated fat 14g, fibre 3g, added sugar 34g, salt 0.69g

A quick pudding that is at its gooey best if you get the cooking time exactly right, but tastes wonderful hot or cold.

Light and Dark Choc Puds

100g bar dark chocolate, chopped
100g/4oz butter, diced
3 large eggs
85g/3oz caster sugar
50g/2oz plain flour
12 squares milk chocolate
Maldon sea salt flakes (optional)

Takes 20–25 minutes • Serves 6

1 Preheat oven to 200°C/Gas 6/fan oven 180°C. Butter and lightly flour six 150ml/ ¼ pint ramekins.
2 Melt the dark chocolate and butter in the microwave on Medium for 2–3 minutes, stirring halfway.
3 Whisk the eggs and sugar until thick enough to leave a ribbon trail when the whisk blades are lifted (about 5 minutes). Stir in the flour, then the melted chocolate mix.
4 Divide among the ramekins and push two milk-chocolate squares into the centre of each. (You can now set them aside for up to 2 hours until you are ready to bake.)
5 Put the ramekins on a baking sheet and bake for 12 minutes exactly. Cool for 5 minutes, turn out on to plates and sprinkle the tops with a pinch of sea salt, if you like.

• Per serving 396 kcalories, protein 7g, carbohydrate 34g, fat 27g, saturated fat 15g, fibre 1g, added sugar 24g, salt 0.39g

If you prefer a chocolate and nut cookie, you can substitute the ginger with the same quantity of your favourite nut.

Ginger Choc-chip Cookies

225g/8oz butter, softened
85g/3oz light muscovado or light soft brown sugar
250g/9oz self-raising flour
2 tbsp golden syrup
1 tsp vanilla extract
100g/4oz dark chocolate drops or dark chocolate, chopped
50g/2oz preserved ginger from a jar or crystallised ginger, roughly chopped

Takes 25–30 minutes, plus chilling and cooling • Makes 20

1 Butter two large baking sheets and line with non-stick parchment. Beat the butter and sugar together until pale and creamy. Stir in the remaining ingredients to make a soft dough. Roll the dough into walnut-sized pieces and space out generously on the baking sheets. Chill for 30 minutes.
2 Meanwhile, preheat oven to 200°C/Gas 6/ fan oven 180°C.
3 Bake the cookies for 12–15 minutes until light golden – they will still feel quite soft in the middle. Leave on the baking sheets for about 5 minutes until firm, then transfer to a rack to cool completely.

• Per cookie 169 kcalories, protein 1g, carbohydrate 20g, fat 10g, saturated fat 6g, fibre 1g, added sugar 11g, salt 0.28g

The low-fat yoghurt will make these just frozen desserts
a slightly less guilty pleasure!

Semifreddo Chocolate Pots

340g jar good-quality chocolate
sauce
2 tbsp brandy
2 tbsp strong black coffee
100g/4oz dessert biscuits
(e.g. langues-de-chat), lightly
broken
2 × 150g cartons low-fat Greek
yoghurt
1 tbsp cocoa powder, to serve

Takes 10 minutes, plus freezing •
Serves 4

1 Pour the chocolate sauce into a large bowl
and microwave on High for 10 seconds until
just softened (or warm gently in a small pan).
Beat to soften further. Mix together the brandy
and coffee, add the biscuits, then toss them
in the liquid.
2 Add the yoghurt to the chocolate sauce
with the biscuits and liquid. Fold together
lightly with a large metal spoon, leaving the
mixture marbled.
3 Spoon into four coffee cups or ramekins
and place in the freezer for 1 hour, or until
just frozen. Dust with cocoa powder
before serving.

• Per serving 384 kcalories, protein 11g, carbohydrate
34g, fat 22g, saturated fat 11g, fibre 1g, added sugar
13g, salt 0.75g

A delicious and stylish way to serve individual fondues, or you can present it in one big bowl for more informal sharing.

Marbled Chocolate Fondue

225g/8oz milk chocolate, chopped
6 tbsp milk
50g/2oz white chocolate, chopped
2 small bananas, peeled and cut into bite-sized chunks
2 nectarines, halved, stoned and cut into wedges
225g/8oz strawberries

Takes 20–30 minutes • Serves 4

1 Melt the milk chocolate with the milk in the microwave for 2–3 minutes, or in a bowl over a pan of hot water. Stir until smooth, then pour into four teacups or small bowls set on plates.

2 Melt the white chocolate as before, without any milk. Drizzle a little white chocolate into each teacup with a spoon and swirl with a skewer or the point of a knife to give a marbled effect. Arrange the fruits on plates, add the teacups and serve immediately.

• Per serving 408 kcalories, protein 7g, carbohydrate 54g, fat 20g, saturated fat 9g, fibre 2g, added sugar 29g, salt 0.18g

If you love your puddings but not the effect they have on your waistline, then this low-fat tiramisu is especially for you.

Blueberry Tiramisu

2 medium eggs, separated
75g/2½oz caster sugar
3 × 250g cartons Quark
3 tbsp skimmed milk
2 tsp vanilla extract
5 tbsp coffee liqueur (e.g. Tia Maria or Kahlúa)
4 tbsp cold strong black coffee
120g/4½oz boudoir biscuits (sponge fingers), halved
75g/2½oz dark chocolate, grated
125g/4½oz blueberries

Takes 30 minutes, plus chilling • Serves 4

1 Whisk the egg yolks and caster sugar until pale and creamy. In a clean bowl, whisk the egg whites to soft peaks. Beat together the Quark, milk and vanilla, and fold in the egg yolk mixture. Gently fold in the egg whites.
2 Mix the liqueur and coffee together in a large bowl. Dip in one batch of biscuits at a time, leaving each in for 20 seconds. Place a layer of these biscuits in the bottoms of four dessert glasses, sprinkle over some grated chocolate and add a few blueberries.
3 Spoon over a little of the Quark mixture then top with more coffee-dipped biscuits. Add more chocolate and blueberries, then top with the remaining Quark mixture. Finish with a sprinkling of chocolate and chill for 30 minutes before serving.

• Per serving 491 kcalories, protein 25g, carbohydrate 54g, fat 16g, saturated fat 6g, fibre 1g, added sugar 39.7g, salt 0.54g

The ultimate nursery food that takes minutes to prepare
so you won't keep hungry children waiting.

Banana Splits

4 bananas
4 scoops vanilla ice cream
4 tbsp good-quality chocolate sauce
2 tbsp flaked toasted almonds

Takes 10 minutes • Serves 4

1 Peel the bananas and cut each one in half lengthways. Overlap two pieces of banana on each of four plates, and top with the scoops of ice cream.
2 Drizzle the chocolate sauce over and around, then scatter with the almonds. Serve immediately.

• Per serving 418 kcalories, protein 8g, carbohydrate 61g, fat 17g, saturated fat 7g, fibre 2g, sugar 56g, salt 0.23g

A timeless, speedy classic that can also be frozen for up to 3 months
– if it doesn't get eaten first!

Choco-nut Fridge Cake

175g/6oz dark chocolate, chopped
175g/6oz butter, diced
2 tbsp golden syrup
100g/4oz digestive biscuits,
lightly crushed
85g/3oz hazelnuts, roasted and
roughly chopped
85g/3oz glacé cherries
85g/3oz raisins
25g/1oz stem ginger, finely chopped
(optional)

Takes 15 minutes, plus chilling and
optional freezing • Cuts into 8 slices

1 Line a 450g/1lb loaf tin with non-stick
parchment. Melt the chocolate and butter in
a bowl over a pan of hot water. Remove from
the heat and stir in the remaining ingredients.
Spoon the mixture into the tin and level the
top. Chill for at least 4 hours, or wrap in foil
and freeze for up to 3 months.
2 Serve cut into slices (if the cake is frozen,
defrost overnight in the fridge first).

• Per slice 466 kcalories, protein 4g, carbohydrate
41g, fat 33g, saturated fat 16g, fibre 2g, added sugar
22.7g, salt 0.6

A divinely light mousse that can be whipped up in moments and, because it contains no egg, it can be enjoyed by everyone.

Creamy Chocolate Mousse

150g/5oz milk chocolate
284ml carton double cream
milk-chocolate shavings,
to decorate

Takes 15 minutes, plus cooling and chilling • Serves 4

1 Chop the chocolate and melt in a bowl over a pan of hot water. Remove and leave to cool slightly.
2 Meanwhile, whip the cream until it just holds its shape, then set 4 tablespoons aside. Fold the melted chocolate into the rest of the whipped cream and divide among four serving glasses. Spoon the reserved whipped cream over the puddings and sprinkle milk-chocolate shavings over the top. Chill until serving time.

• Per serving 589 kcalories, protein 4.6g, carbohydrate 27.1g, fat 52.1g, saturated fat 29.7g, fibre 0.4g, sugar 27.1g, salt 0.14g

Dried cranberries and pistachios give a festive flavour to chocolate brownies, and make delicious homemade Christmas gifts.

Cranberry-pistachio Brownies

2 × 150g bars dark chocolate (preferably 50% cocoa solids), chopped
225g/8oz butter, diced
280g/10oz light muscovado sugar
4 tbsp cranberry juice or milk
4 medium eggs
225g/8oz plain flour
½ tsp ground cinnamon
75–80g pack dried cranberries
100g/4oz pistachios, sliced
icing sugar, for dusting (optional)

Takes 45–55 minutes, plus cooling • Makes 18

1 Preheat oven to 180°C/Gas 4/fan oven 160°C. Butter and base-line a non-stick baking tin (about 31×17×3.5cm/12½×6½ ×1¼in). Melt the chocolate with the butter, sugar and juice or milk, stirring until evenly mixed. Cool slightly, then beat in the eggs one at a time. Fold in the flour, cinnamon and cranberries.
2 Spread half the mixture in the tin, scatter over the nuts, then gently spread the rest of the mixture on top. Bake for 25–30 minutes. Cut into squares in the tin while warm, leave to cool then dust with icing sugar, if using.

• Per brownie 333 kcalories, protein 5g, carbohydrate 39g, fat 18g, saturated fat 9g, fibre 1g, added sugar 27g, salt 0.3g

The unbeatable combination of chocolate and orange makes a gorgeously light and zesty cake.

Jaffa Drizzle Loaf

FOR THE CAKE
140g/5oz butter, softened
225g/8oz self-raising flour
1½ tsp baking powder
225g/8oz golden caster sugar
3 large eggs
6 tbsp milk
finely grated zest of 1 large orange

TO FINISH
3 tbsp orange juice
50g/2oz golden caster sugar
50g/2oz dark chocolate, chopped

Takes 1¼ hours, plus cooling and setting • Cuts into 8–10 slices

1 Preheat oven to 180°C/Gas 4/fan oven 160°C. Butter and base-line a 1.2 litre/2 pint loaf tin. Put all the cake ingredients into a bowl and beat until light and fluffy. Spoon the mix into the tin and level the top. Bake for 40–50 minutes until golden brown and firm to the touch.

2 Meanwhile, heat the orange juice and sugar gently in a small pan, stirring until dissolved. When the cake is cooked, remove it from the oven and spoon over the orange mix. Leave to cool in the tin, then remove and cool completely on a rack.

3 Melt the chocolate in a bowl over a pan of hot water (or in the microwave on Medium for 1–2 minutes). Drizzle over the cake and leave to set before slicing.

• Per slice for 8 410 kcalories, protein 5.9g, carbohydrate 57.2g, fat 19.2g, saturated fat 10.9g, fibre 0.9g, added sugar 38.2g, salt 0.88g

For a really special afternoon tea, it's worth spending a little extra time in the kitchen to create these utterly indulgent éclairs.

Chocolate Éclairs

100g/4oz butter, diced
300ml/½ pint water
140g/5oz plain flour, sifted
4 large eggs, lightly beaten with
a fork

FOR THE FILLING
568ml carton double cream
1 tbsp caster sugar
1 vanilla pod, split lengthways and
seeds scraped out

FOR THE ICING
a knob of butter
100g/4oz dark chocolate, melted

Takes 50 minutes, plus cooling and
setting • Makes 20

1 Preheat oven to 200°C/Gas 6/fan oven 180°C. Grease two baking sheets. Bring the butter and water to the boil. Tip in all the flour, remove from the heat and beat to a soft dough ball. Cool for 5 minutes. Gradually beat in the eggs until a smooth, glossy paste.
2 Spoon into a piping bag with a 2cm/¾in plain nozzle. Pipe 20 éclairs, 8cm/3¼in long, on the baking sheets. Bake for 25–30 minutes, swapping the sheets midway. Slit éclairs halfway along each side, and bake for another 5 minutes until crisp. Cool on racks.
3 Whip the cream, sugar and vanilla seeds until just peaking. Slit the éclairs completely, open them out and spoon in the filling.
4 Make the icing. Stir the butter into the warm melted chocolate, leave to thicken, then spoon over the éclairs and leave to set.

• Per éclair 243 kcalories, protein 3g, carbohydrate 10g, fat 22g, saturated fat 13g, fibre trace, added sugar 4g, salt 0.17g

The refreshing flavour of Lady Grey tea, with its delicate infusions of orange, lemon and bergamot, makes for truly sophisticated biscuits.

Lady Grey Biscuits

140g/5oz butter, softened
100g/4oz light muscovado sugar
2 tbsp Lady Grey tea leaves
50g/2oz dark chocolate, finely chopped
1 large egg, beaten
200g/7oz plain flour

FOR THE ICING
140g/5oz icing sugar
2 tbsp strained Lady Grey tea (strongly brewed)

Takes 35 minutes, plus chilling, cooling and setting • Makes 40

1 Beat the butter and sugar until light and fluffy. Beat in the tea leaves, chocolate and egg, then fold in the flour to make a soft dough. Shape the dough into a sausage about 25cm/10in long, wrap tightly in cling film and chill for about 1 hour until firm.
2 Preheat oven to 190°C/Gas 5/fan oven 170°C. Grease two baking sheets.
3 Cut slices off the roll of dough about 5mm/¼in thick. Place on the baking sheets, spacing them a little apart. Bake for 10–15 minutes until lightly browned, then cool on a rack.
4 Make the icing. Sift the sugar into a bowl, then beat in the tea until you have a smooth icing that is not too thick. Drizzle over each biscuit and leave to set.

• Per biscuit 77 kcalories, protein 0.9g, carbohydrate 11.1g, fat 3.5g, saturated fat 2.1g, fibre 0.2g, sugar 7g, salt 0.06g

Crunchy coconut hides a wonderfully soft and light chocolate cake underneath.

Chocolate Coconut Squares

100g/4oz butter, softened
100g/4oz caster sugar
2 large eggs, beaten
140g/5oz self-raising flour
1 tsp baking powder
2 tbsp cocoa powder
2 tbsp milk
100g/4oz desiccated coconut,
for coating

FOR THE ICING
100g/4oz dark chocolate, chopped
25g/1oz butter
100g/4oz icing sugar, sifted

Takes 40 minutes, plus cooling and
setting • Makes 16

1 Preheat oven to 180°C/Gas 4/fan oven 160°C. Butter and line a 20cm/8in square baking tin. Beat the butter and sugar until pale and creamy. Beat in the eggs, adding 1 tbsp of flour if the mix starts to separate.
2 Sift the flour, baking powder and cocoa over the creamed mixture, then fold in with the milk. Scrape the mixture into the tin and level the top. Bake for 18–20 minutes or until the cake springs back when pressed in the centre. Cool in the tin.
3 Make the icing. Gently heat the chocolate, butter and 4 tbsp water in a pan until melted. Cool slightly, then beat in the icing sugar.
4 Remove the cake from the tin and peel away the paper. Cut into 16 squares. Dip the squares into the icing, then coat with the coconut. Leave to set on a wire rack.

• Per square 225 kcalories, protein 2g, carbohydrate 25g, fat 13g, saturated fat 9g, fibre 1g, sugar 18g, salt 0.34g

*A fantastically easy and speedy cake to make,
and the baking time is worth the wait!*

Cinnamon Nutella Cake

175g/6oz butter, softened
175g/6oz golden caster sugar
3 large eggs, beaten
225g/8oz self-raising flour
1 tsp baking powder
2 tsp ground cinnamon
4 tbsp milk
4 rounded tbsp Nutella or other hazelnut chocolate spread
50g/2oz hazelnuts, roughly chopped

Takes 1½ hours, plus cooling •
Cuts into about 12 slices

1 Preheat oven to 180°C/Gas 4/fan oven 160°C. Butter and line a 20cm/8in cake tin.
2 Put the butter, sugar, eggs, flour, baking powder, cinnamon and milk into a bowl. Beat with a wooden spoon for 2–3 minutes, or with an electric mixer for 1–2 minutes, until light and fluffy.
3 Tip three-quarters of the mixture into the tin, spread it level, then spoon four blobs of Nutella on top. Pile on the remaining mixture, swirl with a skewer, then smooth to cover the Nutella. Sprinkle with the nuts.
4 Bake for 1 hour–1 hour 10 minutes until risen and firm to the touch. Cover the cake with foil if it starts to brown too quickly. Cool in the tin for 10 minutes, turn out and peel off the paper. Cool on a rack before slicing.

• Per slice 320 kcalories, protein 5g, carbohydrate 34g, fat 19g, saturated fat 8g, fibre 1g, added sugar 20g, salt 0.63g

Lusciously light and elegant cookies that make an ideal
accompaniment to after-dinner coffee.

Pecan and Chocolate Clouds

2 large egg whites
a pinch of salt
120g/4½oz golden caster sugar
120g/4½oz pecan nuts, roughly
chopped
150g/5oz dark chocolate (preferably
70% cocoa solids), roughly
chopped
1 tsp vanilla extract

Takes 20–30 minutes, plus cooling •
Makes 32

1 Preheat oven to 180°C/Gas 4/fan oven
160°C. Line two baking sheets with foil.
2 In a large, clean bowl, whisk the egg whites
with the salt until stiff and dry. Gradually whisk
in the sugar a little at a time to make a thick
and glossy meringue. Tip in the pecans and
chocolate, then the vanilla, and fold in gently
with a large metal spoon.
3 Spoon heaped teaspoonfuls of the
meringue mixture, spaced apart, on the lined
baking sheets. Put the sheets in the oven,
then turn it off and leave the cookies for at
least 3 hours or until the oven is cold (you
can leave them overnight). Peel the cookies
carefully from the foil.

• Per cookie 66 kcalories, protein 1g, carbohydrate 7g,
fat 4g, saturated fat 1g, fibre none, added sugar 7g,
salt 0.06g

Gorgeous gooey and fudgy brownies – drizzle them with toffee sauce and you won't be able to keep your hands off them.

Marbled Toffee Brownies

150g/5oz dark chocolate, chopped
175g/6oz butter, diced
250g bag creamy toffees
5 tbsp double cream
4 large eggs
2 tsp vanilla extract
350g/12oz caster sugar
200g/7oz plain flour
1 tsp baking powder
100g/4oz pecan nuts, roughly chopped

Takes 1¼ hours, plus cooling and setting • Makes 18

1 Preheat oven to 180°C/Gas 4/fan oven 160°C. Grease a shallow 28×18cm/11×7in baking tin and line with baking parchment. Melt 100g/4oz of the chocolate with the butter. Melt the toffees with the cream.
2 Lightly beat the eggs with the vanilla, stir into the melted chocolate with the sugar. Sift in the flour and baking powder, mixing lightly. Stir in the pecans. Pour half the mixture into the tin and drizzle over three-quarters of the toffee sauce. Spread over the rest of the brownie mixture. Bake for 40–45 minutes until firm to touch. Leave to cool on a rack.
3 Reheat the remaining toffee sauce, and melt the remaining chocolate. With the tip of a teaspoon, quickly drizzle the toffee sauce over the cake, then repeat with the melted chocolate. Leave to set before cutting.

• Per brownie 369 kcalories, protein 4.1g, carbohydrate 44.5g, fat 20.7g, saturated fat 10.3g, fibre 0.8g, sugar 32.7g, salt 0.41g

This simple traybake works just as well with blueberries or cherries instead of raspberries.

Berry and Chocolate Traybake

375g pack ready-rolled shortcrust pastry
500g carton mascarpone
100g/4oz golden caster sugar
100g/4oz ground almonds
2 large eggs, beaten
250g/9oz raspberries
100g/4oz white chocolate, chopped

Takes 45–50 minutes, plus cooling and optional chilling • Cuts into 16 pieces

1 Preheat oven to 160°C/Gas 3/fan oven 140°C. On a floured surface, roll out the pastry until it is a little thinner and use to line a 30×20cm/12×8in tin or a Swiss roll tin. Line with greaseproof paper, fill with baking beans and bake blind for 10 minutes. Remove the paper and beans, then return the pastry to the oven for a further 5 minutes.

2 Whisk together the mascarpone, sugar, almonds and eggs until well blended. Fold in the raspberries and chocolate, then pour into the tin. Bake for 20–25 minutes until just set and lightly golden. Turn the oven off, prop the door open and leave the traybake to cool gradually. For the best results, chill for at least 1 hour before slicing.

• Per piece 314 kcalories, protein 5g, carbohydrate 19g, fat 25g, saturated fat 12g, fibre 2g, sugar 13g, salt 0.18g

Totally decadent brownies for the dedicated chocoholic,
with bite after bite of delicious dark chocolate.

Chocolate Brownies

375g/13oz dark chocolate, chopped
375g/13oz butter, diced
500g/1lb 2oz caster sugar
6 medium eggs
225g/8oz plain flour

FOR THE TOPPING
140g/5oz dark chocolate, chopped
50g/2oz butter, diced
icing sugar, for dusting

Takes 1¼ hours, plus cooling and
setting • Makes 24

1 Preheat oven to 180°C/Gas 4/fan oven
160°C. Butter and line a 30×21cm/12×8¼in
cake tin. Melt the chocolate with the butter
in a bowl over a pan of hot water (or in the
microwave on Medium for about 5 minutes,
stirring halfway).
2 Beat the sugar and eggs in a bowl. Stir in
the melted chocolate, add the flour and beat
well. Pour into the tin and bake for 40–45
minutes, or until the top looks papery and
feels slightly wobbly. Leave to cool in the tin.
3 For the topping, melt the chocolate with
the butter in a bowl over a pan of hot water
(or in the microwave on Medium for about
1 minute). Stir until smooth, then spread over
the cake. Dust with icing sugar and leave until
set before cutting into squares.

• Per brownie 383 kcalories, protein 4g, carbohydrate
40g, fat 24g, saturated fat 14g, fibre 1g, added sugar
30g, salt 0.39g

These gluten-free ginger biscuits will spice up a coffee morning, but you can use ordinary flour and baking powder if you prefer.

Chocolate Ginger Biscuits

175g/6oz gluten-free flour
1 tsp ground ginger
½ tsp gluten-free baking powder
100g/4oz dairy-free margarine, softened
50g/2oz golden caster sugar
50g/2oz preserved stem ginger, finely chopped
300g bar sugar-free dark chocolate, melted

Takes 35–40 minutes, plus chilling, cooling and setting • Makes 10

1 Preheat oven to 180°C/Gas 4/fan oven 160°C. Lightly grease a baking sheet. Sift the flour, ground ginger and baking powder into a bowl. In a separate bowl, beat the margarine and sugar until pale and creamy. Add the chopped ginger and flour, and stir to form a stiff dough. Wrap in cling film and chill for 30 minutes.
2 On a lightly floured surface, roll out the dough to the thickness of a £2 coin. Using a 6cm/2½in cutter, stamp out 10 discs, dipping the cutter in flour after each disc. Re-roll trimmings for more biscuits. Transfer the biscuits to the baking sheet.
3 Bake for 15–20 minutes until pale golden and just crisp. Carefully transfer to a rack and allow to cool. Drizzle the chocolate over the cooled biscuits and leave to set.

• Per biscuit 341 kcalories, protein 3g, carbohydrate 38g, fat 21g, saturated fat 8g, fibre 2g, sugar 17g, salt 0.29g

A real teatime favourite, full of texture and flavour.

Apricot, Pecan and Choc-chip Loaf

100g/4oz ready-to-eat dried apricots, chopped
150ml/¼ pint unsweetened orange juice
100g/4oz butter, softened
100g/4oz light muscovado sugar
2 large eggs, beaten
100g/4oz ground almonds
175g/6oz self-raising flour
3 tbsp milk
50g/2oz chocolate chips
85g/3oz pecan halves
icing sugar, for dusting

Takes 1¼–1½ hours, plus cooling • Cuts into 12 slices

1 Preheat oven to 180°C/Gas 4/fan oven 160°C. Butter and base-line a 1.2 litre/2 pint loaf tin. Simmer the apricots in a small pan with the orange juice for 5 minutes. Cool.
2 Beat the butter, sugar, eggs, almonds, flour and milk in a bowl until smooth. Stir in the apricots, chocolate chips and two-thirds of the pecans.
3 Spoon into the loaf tin and smooth the top. Scatter over the remaining pecans and bake for 50–60 minutes until firm to the touch and a skewer inserted into the centre comes out clean. Cool for 5 minutes, turn out on to a rack and dust with icing sugar. Leave to cool completely before serving.

• Per slice 307 kcalories, protein 6g, carbohydrate 28g, fat 20g, saturated fat 6g, fibre 2g, sugar 16g, salt 0.36g

Delightfully crumbly chocolate cake that would also be a wonderful warm pudding, served with vanilla ice cream.

Crumbly Chocolate Squares

FOR THE CAKE
175g/6oz butter at room temperature, diced
225g/8oz golden caster sugar
175g/6oz plain flour
3 large eggs
3 tbsp milk
1 tsp baking powder

FOR THE TOPPING
100g/4oz dark chocolate, chopped
100g/4oz light muscovado sugar
85g/3oz mixed chopped nuts
1 tsp ground cinnamon

Takes 1–1¼ hours, plus cooling •
Makes 15

1 Preheat oven to 180°C/Gas 4/ fan oven 160°C. Butter and base-line a 28×18cm/11×7in traybake tin. Put the cake ingredients into a large bowl and beat with an electric mixer until well blended and creamy. Tip the mixture into the tin and spread evenly right into the corners.
2 Top the cake mixture with the chocolate pieces, scattering them evenly. Mix the remaining topping ingredients, scatter them over the chocolate, then press lightly to compact the mixture. Bake for 40 minutes until risen and firm to the touch. Cool in the tin before cutting into squares.

• Per square 294 kcalories, protein 4g, carbohydrate 35g, fat 16g, saturated fat 8g, fibre 1g, added sugar 25g, salt 0.39g

White chocolate gives these muffins a smooth taste, but if you prefer you could substitute it with milk chocolate.

Choc-cherry Muffins

250g/9oz self-raising flour
1 tsp bicarbonate of soda
140g/5oz dried sour cherries
100g bar white chocolate, chopped
100g bar dark chocolate, chopped
100g/4oz golden caster sugar
2 large eggs, beaten
150ml carton natural yoghurt
100g/4oz butter, melted

Takes 30 minutes, plus cooling •
Makes 12

1 Preheat oven to 200°C/Gas 6/fan oven 180°C. Line a 12-hole muffin tin with paper cases. Sift the flour and soda into a large bowl, then stir in the cherries, chocolate and sugar. Add the eggs, yoghurt and butter, and stir to combine. It doesn't matter if the mixture looks lumpy – it's important not to overmix or the muffins will turn out tough.
2 Fill the paper cases and bake for 20 minutes or until risen and golden brown. Transfer to a rack to cool. These are especially delicious eaten slightly warm.

• Per muffin 386 kcalories, protein 5g, carbohydrate 45g, fat 13g, saturated fat 6g, fibre 1g, added sugar 18g, salt 0.73g

An Australian speciality, Lamingtons will delight the tastebuds with their combination of chocolate, vanilla cream and coconut.

Lamingtons

6 large eggs
140g/5oz caster sugar
225g/8oz self-raising flour
5 tbsp hot water
25g/1oz butter, melted

FOR THE VANILLA CREAM
250g/9oz icing sugar, sifted
1 tsp vanilla extract
50g/2oz butter, softened
2 tsp milk

FOR THE ICING
300g/10oz icing sugar
4 tbsp cocoa powder
25g/1oz butter
125ml/4fl oz milk
140g/5oz desiccated coconut

Takes 1½ hours, plus cooling and setting • Makes 16

1 Preheat oven to 180°C/Gas 4/fan oven 160°C. Grease a 23cm/9in square cake tin. Beat the eggs and sugar until pale and thick. Fold in the flour, water and butter. Pour into the tin and bake for 35 minutes until firm. Turn out on to a rack and cool.

2 Whip the vanilla-cream ingredients together until very thick and creamy. Cut the cake into 16, then cut each square horizontally in half and sandwich together with the cream.

3 Sift the sugar and cocoa for the icing into a bowl. Microwave the butter and milk on High for 1 minute until the butter has melted. Stir into the sugar mixture, spoon over each square and lift with a fork so the icing drains off. Put on a rack and sprinkle with the coconut. Leave to set overnight.

• Per square 360 kcalories, protein 4.8g, carbohydrate 57g, fat 14.1g, saturated fat 9g, fibre 1.8g, sugar 46.4g, salt 0.33g

For the purists out there, these brownies are simply unadulterated chocolate heaven!

Best-ever Brownies

185g/6½oz dark chocolate, chopped
185g/6½oz unsalted butter, diced
3 large eggs
275g/9½oz golden caster sugar
85g/3oz plain flour
40g/1½oz cocoa powder
50g/2oz white chocolate, chopped
50g/2oz milk chocolate, chopped

Takes 1 hour, plus cooling • Makes 32

1 Preheat oven to 180°C/Gas 4/fan oven 160°C. Butter and base-line a 20cm/8in square cake tin that is 5cm/2in deep.
2 Melt the chocolate with the butter. Cool. Whisk the eggs and sugar until thick and creamy and double their original volume. Pour over the cooled chocolate and fold together. Sift over the flour and cocoa and fold in. Now stir in the chopped chocolate.
3 Pour into the tin, spread into the corners, and bake for 25 minutes. If it wobbles in the middle, it's not quite done, so bake for another 5 minutes until the top has a shiny, papery crust and the sides begin to come away from the tin. Remove from the tin when completely cold. Cut into quarters, then into four squares and finally into triangles.

• Per triangle 144 kcalories, protein 2g, carbohydrate 17g, fat 8g, saturated fat 5g, fibre 0.5g, added sugar 14g, salt 0.06g

You can't rush a good macaroon, but make them in the morning
and they'll be ready and waiting for afternoon tea!

Coconut and Chocolate Macaroons

1 large egg white
225g/8oz caster sugar
4 tbsp plain flour
225g/8oz coarsely grated fresh
coconut (about 1 coconut)
150g bar dark chocolate, chopped

Takes 50 minutes, plus cooling and
setting • Make 12

1 Preheat oven to 180°C/Gas 4/fan oven 160°C. Line a baking tray with non-stick parchment. Whisk the egg white until stiff, then gradually add the sugar, whisking continuously until thick and glossy. Sift the flour over the egg white, then fold in with the coconut until completely combined.
2 Squash 12 spoonfuls of the mixture on to the lined tray and cut out using an 8cm/3¼in pastry cutter – you may need to do this in two batches. Bake for 15–18 minutes until golden at the edge and just starting to brown on top. Leave to cool, then transfer to a rack.
3 While they are cooling, melt the chocolate in a bowl over a pan of hot water (or in the microwave). Cool slightly then spread over the smooth side of each macaroon. Leave to set in the fridge before serving.

• Per macaroon 206 kcalories, protein 2g, carbohydrate 30g, fat 10g, saturated fat 7g, fibre 2g, sugar 26g, salt 0.03g

Perfect for picnics or teatime, these bars
are bursting with flavour.

Butterscotch Choc Bars

140g/5oz butter, diced
2 large eggs
350g/12oz light muscovado sugar
2 tsp vanilla extract
250g/9oz self-raising flour
100g bar milk chocolate, cut into
large chunks
100g/4oz macadamia or pecan nuts,
coarsely chopped
icing sugar, for dusting

Takes 40–50 minutes, plus cooling •
Makes 12

1 Preheat oven to 180°C/Gas 4/fan oven 160°C. Butter a shallow 24×20cm/9½×8in cake tin.
2 Melt the butter in a small, heavy pan, then leave to cool for 5 minutes. Beat the eggs in a bowl, add the butter, sugar and vanilla, then tip in the flour. Stir in the chocolate chunks and three-quarters of the nuts.
3 Spread the mixture in the tin and scatter the remaining nuts on top. Bake for 25–30 minutes, then cut into 12 bars. Cool and dust with icing sugar before serving.

• Per bar 387 kcalories, protein 5g, carbohydrate 49g, fat 20g, saturated fat 8g, fibre 2g, sugar 35g, salt 0.03g

Mouth-wateringly moist flapjacks that are full of healthy ingredients with a tempting taste of chocolate.

Chocolate-orange Flapjacks

250g/9oz unsalted butter, diced
250g/9oz caster sugar
175g/6oz golden syrup
finely grated zest of 2 oranges
425g/15oz porridge oats
100g/4oz sultanas
100g/4oz ready-to-eat dried apricots, roughly chopped
2 tbsp sunflower seeds
50g/2oz dark chocolate chips
75g/2½ oz dark chocolate, melted

Takes 40–45 minutes, plus cooling and setting • Makes 14

1 Preheat oven to 180°C/Gas 4/fan oven 160°C. Lightly oil and base-line a shallow 30×20cm/12×8in cake tin.
2 In a large pan over a low heat, melt the butter, sugar and syrup with the zest, stirring occasionally. Remove from the heat and stir in the oats, sultanas, apricots and seeds. Cool slightly, then stir in the chocolate chips and spoon into the tin. Level the surface and bake for 20–25 minutes until golden. Mark into 14 bars, leave in the tin until almost cold, then turn out on to a board.
3 Remove the lining paper and break into bars. Spoon the melted chocolate into a piping bag and drizzle the chocolate randomly over the bars. (Or just drizzle the chocolate from a teaspoon.) Leave the chocolate to set before serving.

• Per flapjack 448 kcalories, protein 5g, carbohydrate 65g, fat 20g, saturated fat 12g, fibre 3g, added sugar 34g, salt 0.13g

These chocolate and pecan squares would double up as a divine dessert, served with cream or créme fraîche.

Choco-nut Traybake

225g/8oz dark chocolate, chopped
100g/4oz unsalted butter, diced
85g/3oz caster sugar
4 large eggs, separated
85g/3oz ground almonds
5 tbsp fresh breadcrumbs
140g/5oz pecan halves

Takes 45–50 minutes, plus cooling • Cuts into 12 squares

1 Preheat oven to 180°C/Gas 4/fan oven 160°C. Grease a 25cm/10in square cake tin and line with non-stick parchment. Put the chocolate and butter in a bowl, cover and microwave on High for 30 seconds. Stir, then return to the microwave for 30 seconds until the chocolate has nearly melted. When cool, but still runny, stir in half the sugar and the egg yolks.
2 Whisk the egg whites to firm peaks. Add the remaining sugar and whisk again until glossy. Stir 1 tbsp egg whites into the chocolate along with the almonds and breadcrumbs, then fold in the rest of the egg whites. Transfer to the tin and top with the pecans. Bake for 25–30 minutes. Cool in the tin for 10 minutes, then lift on to a rack to cool completely. Cut into squares to serve.

• Per square 347 kcalories, protein 6g, carbohydrate 25g, fat 26g, saturated fat 9g, fibre 2g, sugar 20g, salt 0.2g

Prunes are the secret ingredient that make this a sticky, moist brownie that you can really sink your teeth into.

Sticky chocolate brownies

140g/5oz dark chocolate (preferably 70% cocoa solids), chopped
290g can prunes in fruit juice, drained and pitted
100g/4oz wholemeal breadcrumbs
1 large egg
2 large egg whites
140g/5oz golden caster sugar
½ tsp vanilla extract
2 tsp mixed seeds (optional)
fromage frais, to serve

Takes 1 hour, plus cooling • Makes 9

1 Preheat oven to 180°C/Gas 4/fan oven 160°C. Line and grease an 18cm/7in square cake tin. Melt the chocolate in a bowl over pan of hot water. Cool, then whiz in a food processor with all the other ingredients except the seeds.
2 Spoon the mixture into the tin and sprinkle mixed seeds over the top if you like. Bake for 35–40 minutes until a skewer inserted in the centre comes out clean. Cool in the tin for a few minutes, then lift out on to a rack. Cool completely, then cut into 9 squares and serve with fromage frais.

• Per brownie 218 kcalories, protein 4g, carbohydrate 41g, fat 5g, saturated fat 3g, fibre 1.5g, sugar 32g, salt 0.3g

The ultimate American cookie is a really indulgent treat,
packed full of chocolate and crunchy peanuts.

American Choc-chunk Cookies

300g/11oz dark chocolate (about
55% cocoa solids)
100g bar milk chocolate
100g/4oz light muscovado sugar
85g/3oz butter, at room temperature
100g/4oz crunchy peanut butter
1 medium egg, beaten
½ tsp vanilla extract
100g/4oz self-raising flour
100g/4oz large salted roasted
peanuts

Takes 40–50 minutes, plus cooling •
Makes 12

1 Preheat oven to 180°C/Gas 4/fan oven
160°C. Chop 200g/7oz of the dark
chocolate into rough chunks, then the milk
chocolate, but keep separate. Chop and melt
the remaining dark chocolate, then beat in
the sugar, butter, peanut butter, egg and
vanilla until well mixed. Stir in the flour, milk
chocolate chunks, nuts and half the dark
chocolate chunks.
2 Drop big spoonfuls in 12 piles on to two
or three baking sheets, leaving room for the
cookies to spread. Press the remaining dark
chocolate chunks into the cookies. Bake for
10–12 minutes until tinged around the edges
(but soft in the middle). Let them cool and
firm up on the baking sheets, then lift off with
a spatula on to a rack and leave until cold.

• Per cookie 381 kcalories, protein 7g, carbohydrate
36g, fat 24g, saturated fat 10g, fibre 2g, added sugar
27g, salt 0.42g

A classic, traditional English cake that is perfect with a steaming mug of tea on a cold winter's day.

Chocolate Malt Cake

400g/14oz dark chocolate, chopped
175g/6oz unsalted butter, diced
6 tbsp malted food-drink powder
(e.g. Ovaltine)
3 medium eggs
175g/6oz light muscovado sugar
2 tsp vanilla extract
140g/5oz wholemeal self-raising
flour
icing sugar, for dusting

Takes 1 hour, plus cooling • Cuts into
16 squares

1 Preheat oven to 190°C/Gas 5/fan oven 170°C. Butter a 20cm/8in square cake tin and line with greaseproof paper. Melt 175g/6oz of the chocolate with the butter in a bowl over a pan of hot water.
2 Blend the malted food drink with 2 tbsp water. In another bowl, beat the eggs and sugar until thick and foamy. Stir in the melted chocolate, vanilla and malted food-drink mixture.
3 Sift the flour into the bowl, then tip in the grains from the sieve and fold in the remaining chocolate pieces. Spoon into the tin and bake for 40 minutes until risen and just firm. Turn the cake out on to a wire rack and leave to cool. Serve cut into squares, dusted with icing sugar.

• Per square 335 kcalories, protein 5g, carbohydrate 42g, fat 18g, saturated fat 11g, fibre 1g, sugar 34g, salt 0.09g

These gorgeous, gooey brownies are the real thing, packed with nuts and loaded with dark chocolate.

Gooey Chocolate Brownies

2 tbsp Nutella or other hazelnut chocolate spread, plus extra to serve
2 tbsp hot water
100g/3½oz butter, softened
200g/7oz caster sugar
2 medium eggs, beaten
1 tsp vanilla extract
90g/3oz self-raising flour
100g/3½oz walnuts or pecan nuts, chopped
140g/5oz dark chocolate, cut into chunks

Takes 1 hour, plus cooling • Makes 12

1 Preheat oven to 160°C/Gas 3/ fan oven 140°C. Lightly grease and line a 28×18cm/11×7in cake tin. In a small bowl, beat the Nutella with the hot water until smooth. In a separate bowl, cream together the butter and sugar until pale. Stir the chocolate-spread mixture, eggs and vanilla into the creamed mixture and beat until smooth. (To save time, you could do all of this in a food processor.)
2 Fold in the flour, nuts and 100g/3½oz of the chocolate chunks and stir until well combined. Spoon into the tin and level the surface. Sprinkle over the remaining chocolate chunks and bake for 40 minutes. Leave to cool completely in the tin, then cut into 12 squares. To serve, top with Nutella.

• Per brownie 296 kcalories, protein 4g, carbohydrate 33g, fat 18g, saturated fat 7g, fibre 1g, added sugar 24g, salt 0.26g

Bursting with milk chocolate and nuts, these fabulous flapjacks
make a delicious lunchbox or teatime treat.

Chunky Chocolate-nut Flapjacks

225g/8oz oats
25g/1oz desiccated coconut
140g/5oz butter, cut into pieces
50g/2oz light muscovado sugar
5 tbsp golden syrup
100g/4oz brazil nuts (or cashews), cut into large chunks
50g/2oz almonds, cut into large chunks
85g/3oz good-quality dark chocolate, broken into large pieces

Takes 45 minutes •
Makes 12

1 Preheat the oven to 180°C/Gas 4/fan oven 160°C. Lightly butter a 23cm/9in square tin and line the base. Mix together the oats and coconut.
2 Put the butter, sugar and syrup in a pan, cook over a low heat, stirring occasionally, until the butter has melted and the sugar dissolved. Remove from the heat and stir in the oat and coconut mixture. Spoon into the tin and press down evenly. Scatter over the nuts and press lightly into the mixture. Stick the chunks of chocolate among the nuts. Bake for 25–30 minutes, or until a pale golden colour.
3 Mark into bars or squares with the back of a knife while still warm, then allow to cool completely before cutting through and removing from the tin.

• Per flapjack 325 kcalories, protein 5g, carbohydrate 28g, fat 22g, saturated fat 10g, fibre 2g, added sugar 15g, salt 0.3g

These light and fluffy muffins earn their place at the dinner table when served dripping with hot chocolate custard.

Muffins with Chocolate Custard

1 tbsp cocoa powder
100g/4oz self-raising flour
½ tsp bicarbonate of soda
50g/2oz golden caster sugar
100ml/3½fl oz skimmed milk
1 large egg
2 tbsp sunflower oil

FOR THE CUSTARD
2 × 150g pots low-fat custard
25g/1oz dark chocolate, chopped

Takes 30 minutes • Serves 6

1 Preheat oven to 170°C/Gas 3/fan oven 150°C. Brush 6 holes of a muffin tin with a drop of oil. Sift the cocoa into a large bowl, add the rest of the dry ingredients and stir to combine. Make a well in the centre.
2 Beat the milk, egg and oil together in a jug, pour into the well, then stir quickly to make a batter. Spoon into the muffin tin and bake for 15 minutes or until risen and firm to the touch.
3 Heat the custard according to its instructions, tip in the chopped chocolate and stir until smooth. Turn the puddings into bowls and pour over the custard.

• Per serving 215 kcalories, protein 5g, carbohydrate 32g, fat 8g, saturated fat 2g, fibre 1g, sugar 17g, salt 0.59g

An irresistible combination of flavours, perfect for peaches and best served warm simply with cream or ice cream.

Chocolate Almond Peaches

4 large, ripe peaches
2 oranges
3 tbsp marsala, Madeira or sherry
50g/2oz butter, softened
50g/2oz golden caster sugar
50g/2oz ground almonds
1 large egg, beaten
25g/1oz dark chocolate, chopped
2 tbsp flaked almonds
thick cream or vanilla ice cream, to serve

Takes 1 hour • Serves 4 (easily doubled)

1 Preheat oven to 180°C/Gas 4/fan oven 160°C. Halve and stone the peaches. Using a teaspoon, scoop out a little flesh from the centre of each peach half, then chop. Finely grate the zest from one orange and mix with the chopped peach flesh. Squeeze the juice from both oranges and mix with the alcohol.
2 Beat the butter and sugar together for about 3 minutes until light and fluffy. Stir in the ground almonds, egg, chopped peach flesh and orange zest, and the chocolate.
3 Sit the peach halves, cut-side up, in one layer in a shallow ovenproof dish. Spoon the filling into each half. Sprinkle with the flaked almonds and the orange-juice mixture.
4 Bake for 35–40 minutes until the peaches are tender and the filling is lightly browned.

• Per serving 399 kcalories, protein 8g, carbohydrate 35g, fat 25g, saturated fat 9g, fibre 5g, added sugar 17g, salt 0.31g

A juicy orange makes a zesty, moist cake that is delicious dusted with cocoa powder and served with luxurious vanilla ice cream.

Whole Orange and Chocolate Cake

1 small orange (about 225g/8oz), halved and pips removed
100g/4oz self-raising flour
1 tsp baking powder
1 tsp ground cinnamon
1 tsp ground coriander
2 tbsp cocoa powder
100g/4oz ground almonds
175g/6oz butter, softened
175g/6oz light muscovado sugar
4 large eggs, separated
vanilla ice cream, to serve

Takes 2¼ hours, plus cooling • Cuts into 12 slices

1 Put the orange in a pan, cover with water and bring to the boil. Simmer, partly covered, for 1 hour, drain and leave until cool.
2 Preheat oven to 180°C/Gas 4/fan oven 160°C. Butter and base-line a 22–23cm/8½–9 in round cake tin.
3 Chop the orange (without peeling). Work to a rough purée in a food processor. Sift the flour, baking powder, spices and cocoa into a bowl. Stir in the almonds.
4 Beat the butter and sugar until light and fluffy. Beat in the egg yolks and orange purée, then fold in the flour mix. Beat the egg whites until stiff, then fold gently into the cake mix in two batches.
5 Pour into the tin and bake for 40–45 minutes until firm. Cool for 5 minutes, turn out and serve warm, with ice cream.

• Per slice 285 kcalories, protein 5g, carbohydrate 24g, fat 19g, saturated fat 9g, fibre 1g, sugar 16g, salt 0.52g

Paradise on a plate – a rich and decadent delight.

Heavenly Chocolate Pudding

100g/4oz butter, diced
2 tbsp golden syrup
100g/4oz dark muscovado sugar
150ml/¼ pint milk
1 egg (large or medium), beaten
1 heaped tbsp cocoa powder
225g/8oz self-raising flour
1 tsp ground cinnamon
¼ tsp bicarbonate of soda

FOR THE SAUCE
100g/4oz dark chocolate, chopped
4 tbsp milk
4 tbsp whipping or double cream
1 tbsp golden syrup

Takes 1½ hours • Serves 6

1 Butter a 1.2 litre/2 pint pudding basin and line the bottom with a disc of buttered greaseproof paper.
2 Melt the butter, syrup and sugar in a pan. Remove from the heat and stir in the milk and egg. Add the cocoa to the flour, then tip this mixture into the pan with the cinnamon and soda.
3 Pour the mixture into the pudding basin, cover tightly with foil and steam for 1¼ hours. Just before the end, heat the sauce ingredients until melted, stirring all the time.
4 Turn the pudding out (run a knife around the inside of the bowl if necessary) and discard the paper disc. Pour the sauce over the top and serve immediately.

• Per serving 485 kcalories, protein 6.5g, carbohydrate 62.2g, fat 25g, saturated fat 14.7g, fibre 1.7g, sugar 35.9, salt 0.86g

A sophisticated and wicked variation on
bread and butter pudding.

Chocolate Croissant Pudding

4 croissants
100g/4oz dark chocolate, chopped
142ml carton double cream
300ml/½ pint milk
4 tbsp dark rum or brandy
100g/4oz caster sugar
85g/3oz butter
a pinch of ground cinnamon
3 large eggs

TO SERVE
icing sugar, for dusting
single cream

Take 50–55 minutes, plus standing •
Serves 6

1 Preheat oven to 180°C/Gas 4/fan oven 160°C. Lightly butter a 1.2 litre/2 pint gratin dish. Cut the croissants into strips with scissors, and scatter them haphazardly in the dish.
2 In a bowl over a pan of hot water, heat all the other ingredients except the eggs, stirring well until the chocolate has melted.
3 Whisk the eggs in a separate bowl, then pour in the chocolate mixture, whisking constantly until everything is well mixed. Pour the mixture evenly over the croissants and gently press the croissants down with a fork. Leave to stand for 10 minutes.
4 Bake the pudding for 30–35 minutes until the top is crunchy and the inside soft and squidgy. Leave to stand for 10 minutes, then dust with icing sugar and serve with cream.

• Per serving 577 kcalories, protein 9g, carbohydrate 44g, fat 39g, saturated fat 21g, fibre 1g, added sugar 27g, salt 0.78g

For a really show-stopping pudding, try this exquisite combination of oozing, smooth chocolate and crunchy pecans.

Chocolate Pecan Fondants

cocoa powder, for dusting
150g bar dark chocolate (at least 50% cocoa solids), chopped
50g/2oz butter, diced
1 large egg, beaten
2 tbsp plain flour
2 tbsp pecan nuts, toasted and very finely chopped
1 tbsp golden caster sugar
a pinch of salt
ice cream, to serve

Takes 40 minutes • Serves 2

1 Preheat oven to 220°C/Gas 7/fan oven 200°C. Butter two individual pudding basins (each about 200ml/7fl oz), then dust generously with cocoa powder.
2 Melt the chocolate with the butter until smooth. Gradually stir in the egg, then the flour, nuts, sugar and salt. Beat gently until everything is combined but still runny.
3 Divide the mixture between the pudding basins. (These can now be chilled for up to a day ahead.) Bake for 15 minutes, or 18 minutes if chilled. Turn out on to small plates and serve with ice cream. Fondants should be cooked on the outside and molten in the middle.

• Per serving 847 kcalories, protein 12g, carbohydrate 56g, fat 65g, saturated fat 32g, fibre 6g, sugar 30g, salt 0.54g

A traditional British pud that is perfect following
a warming winter roast.

Sticky Choccy Pudding

100g/4oz butter, softened
175g/6oz dark muscovado sugar
3 large eggs, beaten
225g/8oz self-raising flour
150ml/¼ pint milk
1 tsp ground cinnamon
140g/5oz stoned dates, chopped
85g/3oz dark chocolate, chopped
50g/2oz pecan halves
single cream, to serve

FOR THE SAUCE
175g/6oz butter, diced
175g/6oz golden syrup
2 tbsp dark muscovado sugar

Takes 40 minutes • Serves 8

1 Butter a 1.2 litre/2 pint pudding basin.
Put the butter, sugar, eggs, flour, milk and
cinnamon in a bowl and beat until light and
fluffy. Stir in the dates, chocolate and pecans,
spoon into the pudding basin and cover
tightly with cling film.
2 Pierce the cling film several times and
microwave on Medium for 12–15 minutes,
until firm to touch. If you insert a skewer in the
centre of the pudding it should come out
clean, apart from traces of melted chocolate.
Leave to stand for 5 minutes.
3 Meanwhile, put the sauce ingredients in a
pan and bring to the boil. Stir to melt the
butter. Simmer for 1–2 minutes until syrupy.
4 Turn the pudding out on to a plate and pour
over some of the sauce. Serve with cream
and the remaining sauce.

• Per serving 693 kcalories, protein 7g, carbohydrate
85g, fat 39g, saturated fat 21g, fibre 2g, added sugar
52g, salt 1.14g

Abracadabra and a spoonful of coconut gives this enchanting chocolate cake a creamy, nutty flavour.

Magic Choco-nut Pudding

FOR THE SPONGE
150g/5oz butter, at room temperature
3 medium eggs
150g/5oz caster sugar
100g/4oz self-raising flour
25g/1oz cocoa powder
1 tsp baking powder
pinch of salt
50g/2oz creamed coconut, grated
85g/3oz dark chocolate, chopped
icing sugar, to serve

FOR THE SAUCE
25g/1oz cocoa powder
4 tbsp boiling water
85g/3oz caster sugar
400ml can coconut milk

Takes 1 hour • Serves 6

1 Preheat oven to 180°C/Gas 4/fan oven 160°C. Butter a 1.7 litre/3 pint baking dish that is no more than 7.5cm/3in deep. Set the dish on a baking sheet.
2 Using an electric mixer, beat all the sponge ingredients, except the chocolate, for 2 minutes. Gently stir in the chocolate, then spoon into the dish and spread level.
3 For the sauce, mix the cocoa with the water in a jug. Gradually stir in the sugar and coconut milk. Pour over the pudding and bake for 40 minutes, or until the sponge is firm to touch. Leave for 5 minutes, then sift with icing sugar before serving.

• Per serving 609 kcalories, protein 8g, carbohydrate 69g, fat 35g, saturated fat 22g, fibre 3g, added sugar 41g, salt 1.55g

If you want to ease your conscience as you eat this brownie, serve it with natural yoghurt or half-fat créme fraîche instead of cream.

Chocolate Brownie Cake

100g/4oz butter
175g/6oz caster sugar
75g/2½oz soft brown or light muscovado sugar
125g/4½oz chocolate (dark or milk), chopped
1 tbsp golden syrup
2 large eggs, beaten
1 tsp vanilla extract
100g/4oz plain flour
½ tsp baking powder
2 tbsp cocoa powder
fresh fruit and double cream, to serve

Takes 1 hour • Serves 6–8

1 Preheat oven to 180°C/Gas 4/fan oven 160°C. Grease and line a 20cm/8in round cake tin.
2 Place the butter, caster sugar, brown sugar, chocolate and golden syrup in a pan and melt gently over a low heat until smooth. Remove from the heat, add the eggs, vanilla, flour, baking powder and cocoa and mix thoroughly.
3 Pour into the tin and bake for 25–30 minutes. Allow to cool in the tin for 10–15 minutes, then cut into wedges and serve warm with fresh fruit and cream.

• Per serving for 6 504 kcalories, protein 5.3g, carbohydrate 73.7g, fat 22.9g, saturated fat 13g, fibre 1.4g, sugar 59.4g, salt 0.5g

Sometimes, when it comes to chocolate, simplicity is key. These luxurious chocolate puddings need no dressing up.

Melting Chocolate Puddings

140g/5oz dark chocolate, chopped
140g/5oz unsalted butter, diced
3 large eggs
3 large egg yolks
85g/3oz golden caster sugar
25g/1oz plain flour
vanilla ice cream or single cream, to serve

Takes 35 minutes • Serves 6

1 Preheat oven to 180°C/Gas 4/fan oven 160°C. Butter six 175ml/6 fl oz dariole moulds and stand them on a baking sheet. Melt the chocolate and butter in a bowl over a pan of hot water (or in the microwave on High for 3 minutes).
2 Beat the whole eggs, yolks and sugar with an electric mixer for about 3 minutes until pale. With the mixer on medium speed, whisk in the melted chocolate. Gently fold in the flour, then divide among the moulds. Bake for 10–12 minutes until risen, but still flat on top and not quite firm. Loosen the edges with a round-bladed knife and turn out immediately. Serve with ice cream or cream.

• Per serving 440 kcalories, protein 7g, carbohydrate 36g, fat 31g, saturated fat 17g, fibre 1g, added sugar 29g, salt 0.11g

You can use any dried or glacé fruits that you wish in these chocolate rounds, but, for best effect, make sure they are a mix of colours.

Tutti-frutti Rounds

200g bar white chocolate, chopped
½ × 250g pack butter, diced
6 rich tea biscuits or 12 rich tea fingers, broken into pieces
4 green glacé cherries or angelica strips, rinsed and dried
50g/2oz dried cranberries
2 tbsp raisins

Takes 20–30 minutes, plus chilling •
Makes 32

1 Melt the chocolate and butter until smooth. Cool, stirring once or twice.
2 Crush the biscuits in a large plastic bag with a rolling pin. Don't crush them completely – they should still have some crunch.
3 Cut the cherries or angelica into pieces the same size as the cranberries and raisins. Stir the biscuits and all the fruits into the melted chocolate and butter, then chill for about 2 hours until almost solid.
4 Scoop half the chilled mixture onto a sheet of cling film and shape into a long roll. Wrap the roll in the film and roll into a sausage the diameter of a £2 coin. Repeat with remaining mixture, using another sheet of cling film. Chill overnight to firm up. Unwrap and cut each roll into 16 rounds with a serrated knife.

• Per round 76 kcalories, protein 1g, carbohydrate 7g, fat 5g, saturated fat 2g, fibre none, added sugar 3g, salt 0.11g

For a child's version of this sundae, omit the coffee and
use chocolate instead of vanilla ice cream.

Iced Mocha Sundae

1 shot cold espresso coffee or
2 tbsp cold strong black coffee
200ml/7fl oz full-fat milk, chilled
3 scoops vanilla or chocolate
ice cream
2 ice cubes
1 chocolate brownie or chocolate
chip cookie

Takes 10 minutes • Serves 1

1 Pour the coffee and milk into a blender.
Add 2 scoops of ice cream and the ice
cubes, then blitz until the consistency of
a smoothie. Pour straight into a tall glass.
2 Top with the last scoop of ice cream and
crumble over the brownie or cookie to finish.

• Per serving 575 kcalories, protein 14g,
carbohydrate 66g, fat 30g, saturated fat 19g, fibre 1g,
added sugar 36g, salt 0.70g

Homemade truffles make a delicious and thoughtful gift,
and these chocolates will store in the fridge for 3 days.

Chocolate Truffles

284ml carton double cream
50g/2oz unsalted butter, diced
280g/10oz dark chocolate
(preferably 70% cocoa solids),
chopped

FLAVOURINGS
bourbon
orange-flavoured liqueur
coconut rum
grated zest and juice of 1 orange

COATINGS
crushed shelled pistachios
lightly toasted desiccated coconut
cocoa powder
dark, milk or white chocolate,
melted

Takes 35 minutes, plus cooling and
chilling • Makes 50

1 Gently heat the cream and butter until
the butter melts and the cream reaches
simmering point. Pour over the chocolate in
a bowl and stir until smooth. Leave plain,
or divide among bowls and mix in flavourings
to taste, 1 teaspoon at a time. Cool and chill
for at least 4 hours.
2 Shape the truffles. Scoop the mixture with
a melon baller dipped in hot water and drop
on to non-stick parchment, or lightly coat your
palms in sunflower oil and roll by hand.
3 Immediately after shaping, gently roll the
truffles in pistachios, coconut or cocoa. For
a chocolate coating, pick up one truffle at a
time with a fork and spoon melted chocolate
over to coat.
4 Chill truffles on parchment until firm, then
store in an airtight container in the fridge.

• Per truffle 67 kcalories, protein 1g, carbohydrate 3g,
fat 6g, saturated fat 3g, fibre none, sugar 2g, salt none

A really comforting drink on a cold day or after a long wintry walk.
Collapse on the sofa and enjoy.

Deluxe Hot Chocolate

600ml/1 pint milk
142ml carton double cream
100g/4oz chocolate (dark 70%
cocoa solids or milk chocolate,
according to taste), chopped
2–3 tbsp brandy (optional)

TO SERVE
mini marshmallows
a little grated chocolate

Takes 10 minutes • Serves 4

1 Pour the milk and cream into a pan and
add your choice of chopped chocolate.
Bring gently to the boil, whisking until smooth.
Add the brandy (if using) and whisk to mix.
2 Serve in individual mugs topped with mini
marshmallows and grated chocolate.

• Per serving 437 kcalories, protein 8g, carbohydrate
29g, fat 33g, saturated fat 18g, fibre 2g, added sugar
13g, salt 0.19g

Fantastically easy cheat's recipe that works just as well as
a dessert in a bowl with wafers.

Rocky-road Cones

2 large scoops chocolate ice cream
2 chocolate fudge bars
a handful of baby marshmallows
a handful of toasted almonds
4 ice-cream cones

Takes 10 minutes, plus softening •
Serves 4

1 Soften the ice cream in the fridge for
about 20 minutes, then beat until slushy.
Roughly chop the fudge bars.
2 Mix the fudge bars, marshmallows and
toasted almonds into the ice cream, tip into
an ice-cream container and refreeze until firm.
To serve, scoop into ice-cream cones.

• Per serving 326 kcalories, protein 5g, carbohydrate
51.1g, fat 12.8g, saturated fat 5.8g, fibre 0.6g,
sugar 45.5g, salt 0.22g

The easiest truffles that make an impressive gift at Easter, Christmas or on any other occasion.

Chocolate Biscuit Truffles

150g/5oz white chocolate, chopped
150g/5oz dark chocolate, chopped
50g/2oz unsalted butter, diced
142ml carton double cream
4 shortbread fingers or biscuits, roughly crumbled
85g/3oz dried fruit (e.g. chopped apricots and cranberries)
finely grated zest of 1 large orange
icing sugar and cocoa powder, for rolling

Takes 25 minutes, plus cooling and chilling • Makes about 30

1 Put the white and dark chocolates in separate bowls and divide the butter between them. Scald the cream and pour half into each bowl. Leave for about 1 minute, then stir until melted and smooth. Cool.
2 Divide the shortbread, fruit and orange zest between the bowls, stir, then chill for at least 4 hours until firm.
3 Scoop the mixtures with a teaspoon, and form into small truffles. Sift icing sugar on to a plate and roll the white truffles in it. Do the same with the cocoa and the dark truffles. Chill until needed, for up to 24 hours.

• Per truffle 118 kcalories, protein 1g, carbohydrate 12g, fat 8g, saturated fat 5g, fibre 1g, sugar 10g, salt 0.04g

For added spice, stir the drink with a cinammon stick and leave it in the mug to infuse as you drink.

Spiced Hot Chocolate

600ml/1 pint milk
85g/3oz dark chocolate
ground cinnamon, for sprinkling

Takes 10 minutes • Serves 4

1 Pour the milk into a pan and break in the chocolate. Heat gently, stirring occasionally, until the chocolate melts. Sprinkle in a couple of pinches of cinnamon.
2 Take off the heat and blend with a hand blender until frothy. Pour into mugs or tea glasses.

• Per serving 179 kcalories, protein 6g, carbohydrate 21g, fat 9g, saturated fat 5g, fibre 1g, added sugar 13g, salt 0.17g

If you don't have a microwave, you can melt the chocolate and butter almost as quickly over a pan of boiling water.

Chocolate Salami

250g/9oz dark chocolate, chopped
100g/4oz butter, diced
3 tbsp clear honey
100g/4oz ground almonds
100g/4oz dried apricots, finely chopped
50g/2oz toasted chopped nuts
225g/8oz amaretti biscuits, finely crushed

Takes 20 minutes, plus chilling •
Cuts into 25 slices

1 Microwave the chocolate, butter and honey on Medium for 3–4 minutes. Stir until smooth, add the almonds, apricots, nuts and three-quarters of the biscuits. Cool. Chill for 1–2 hours until firm enough to shape.
2 Spoon the chocolate mixture along the length of a sheet of greaseproof paper, then wrap around it and roll into a neat sausage about 25cm/10in long. Chill for 30 minutes.
3 Spread the remaining biscuits over a second sheet of greaseproof paper. Unwrap the roll and roll it over the biscuit crumbs so that it is coated evenly. Wrap in greaseproof paper again, then overwrap tightly with foil, twisting the ends to seal. Chill until firm, preferably overnight.
4 To serve, unwrap the roll and cut into 25 thin slices with a sharp knife.

• Per slice 166 kcalories, protein 2.6g, carbohydrate 16.7g, fat 10.3g, saturated fat 4.3g, fibre 1.1g, sugar 12.2g, salt 0.17g

Serve these speedy cocktails as a divinely decadent end
to a dinner party.

Mocha Cocktails

142ml carton double cream
5 tbsp creamy liqueur
(e.g. Baileys)
125ml/4fl oz cold strong
black coffee
4 tbsp vodka
4 tbsp coffee liqueur (e.g. Tia Maria
or Kahlúa)

TO SERVE
coffee beans, for decoration
chocolate or almond biscotti

Takes 15 minutes • Serves 4

1 Lightly whip the cream until slightly
thickened, then stir in the chocolate liqueur
and whip a little more, or thin if necessary
with a little water, to get a thick, creamy
pouring consistency.
2 Divide the coffee, vodka and coffee liqueur
among four glasses. Carefully spoon over the
cream and sprinkle with a few coffee beans.
Serve immediately, with biscotti.

• Per cocktail 360 kcalories, protein 1g, carbohydrate
11g, fat 27g, saturated fat 11g, fibre none, added
sugar 11g, salt 0.12g

Index

Picture credits and recipe credits

BBC Worldwide would like to thank the following for providing photographs. While every effort has been made to trace and acknowledge all photographers, we would like to apologize should there be any errors or omissions.

Marie-Louise Avery p57, p69, p77, p137, p189, p195; Iain Bagwell p71, p93; Steve Baxter p65, p121, p123, p151; Martin Brigdale p135; Linda Burgess p37, p63, p81, p83, p129; Peter Cassidy p47, p103, p113, p119, p149, p203, p207; Jean Cazals p35, p45, p101, p139, p185, p193, p209; Gus Filgate p43, p153; Will Heap p145, p163; Dave King p95; Lisa Linder p23; William Lingwood p15, p197; Tim Macpherson p205; Gareth Morgans p17, p29, p97, p159, p175; David Munns p11, p33, p61, p109, p127, p181, p191, p211; Myles New p39, p55, p141, p147, p199; Lis Parsons p111; Michael Paul p167; William Reavell p161; Craig Robertson p53, p105; Roger Stowell p49, p51, p67, p73, p87, p183; Debi Treloar p179; Ian Wallace p107; Cameron Watt p79; Philip Webb p21, p25, p31, p75, p91,p125, p131, p157, p173; Simon Wheeler p13, p15, p19, p59, p143, p155, p177; Geoff Wilkinson p41, p99, p115; Tim Young p89; Elizabeth Zeschin p27, p133, p201

All the recipes in this book have been created by the editorial team on *BBC Good Food Magazine*:

Lorna Brash, Sara Buenfeld, Mary Cadogan, Barney Desmazery, Jane Hornby, Emma Lewis, Kate Moseley, Orlando Murrin, Vicky